About the Author

Marjorie Wilkins Campbell (1902–1986) was born in London, England, and immigrated with her family to the Qu'Appelle Valley in Saskatchewan in 1904. After seven years pioneering on the farm, the Campbell family moved to Swift Current.

A distinguished journalist, Marjorie Wilkins Campbell contributed to numerous magazines, including *Maclean's*, *Saturday Night*, *National Geographic*, and *Magazine Digest*. She was also an award-winning author, penning a total of twelve books, many of which focussed on the early exploration of the West and the Canadian fur trade. Two of her books were honoured with the prestigious Governor General's Award: *The Saskatchewan* won the prize for creative non-fiction in 1950 and *The Nor'Westers* won the prize for juvenile literature in 1954.

Marjorie Wilkins Campbell became a member of the Order of Canada in 1978 for her contribution to our knowledge of Canadian history.

" . . . the voyageurs did the loading while Fraser
supervised the entire project, not daring to leave
a single essential pack behind."

The Savage River

Seventy-one Days with Simon Fraser

Marjorie Wilkins Campbell

FIFTH
HOUSE

Cover and interior design by Mark Shaver / Icon Communications
Front cover photograph by Digital Vision Photography
Interior illustrations by James Delainey
Map by Toby Foord
Scans by St. Solo Computer Graphics
Edited by Bobbi Coulter
Proofread by Peggy Lipinski

The publisher gratefully acknowledges the support of The Canada Council for the Arts and the Department of Canadian Heritage. We acknowledge the financial support of the Government of Canada through the Book Publishing Industry Development Program (BPIDP) for our publishing activities.   Canada Council   Conseil des Arts
                                                                              for the Arts   du Canada

Printed in Canada by Friesens

03 04 05 06 07 / 5 4 3 2 1

NATIONAL LIBRARY OF CANADA CATALOGUING IN PUBLICATION DATA

Campbell, Marjorie Wilkins, 1902–1986
    The savage river : seventy-one days with Simon Fraser / Marjorie Wilkins Campbell.

    Includes index.
    ISBN 1-894856-24-4

    1. Fraser, Simon, 1776–1862. 2. Fraser River (B.C.)—Discovery and exploration. I. Title.
    FC3212.1.F73C35 2003   971.1'302   C2002-911482-9
    F1060.7.F7C35 2003

Fifth House Ltd.   First published in the United States
A Fitzhenry & Whiteside Company   in 2003 by
1511-1800 4 St. SW   Fitzhenry & Whiteside
Calgary, Alberta, Canada   121 Harvard Avenue, Suite 2
T2S 2S5   Allston, MA 02134

1-800-387-9776
www.fitzhenry.ca

Contents

Author's Note

Simon Fraser's name is already linked with that of Dr. W. Kaye Lambe, who has edited and introduced his journals and letters. For Dr. Lamb's thorough scholarship and insight, all who are interested in Fraser's life and times owe a warm and respectful debt of gratitude. It is a debt I am happy to acknowledge.

M.E.W.C.
Toronto, 1968

Remembering Blair Fraser—1909–1968

With his fellow voyagers he re-explored Simon Fraser's route to the Pacific slope.

Foreword

When it appeared in 1968, *The Savage River* was the thirty-third volume in the *Great Stories of Canada* series. This long-running series of books, launched in 1953, was an attempt by the publisher Macmillan of Canada to interest youngsters in the history of their country by presenting it in the form of dramatic adventure stories. What the books lacked in the way of analysis, they made up for in exciting narrative and heroic characters. Some of Canada's most popular writers contributed to the series, including Pierre Berton, Roderick Haig-Brown, Thomas Raddall, and Joseph Schull.

Marjorie Wilkins Campbell (1902–1986) deserves her place among this talented company. The daughter of English immigrant parents, Campbell grew up in Saskatchewan's Qu'Appelle Valley, where she absorbed the landscape and stories of the western fur country from a young age. Later, as a Toronto-based editor and writer, she produced award-winning books for a variety of audiences. The Governor General's Awards are Canada's highest honour for writers, and Campbell won two of them. Her book about the Saskatchewan River (called, simply, *The Saskatchewan*) won the non-fiction prize in 1950, while her book *The Nor'Westers* won the prize for juvenile literature in 1954. Whereas *The Nor'Westers* presents the entire history of the Montreal company that competed to control the Canadian fur trade in the early decades of the nineteenth century, *The Savage River* narrows the focus down to a single member of the company, Simon Fraser, and a single event, his tortuous descent of one of the wildest rivers in North America.

By the time Fraser made the trip that is described in this book, the North West Company had extended its network of trading posts right across the continent. Fraser himself had crossed the Rocky Mountains and opened the first post in British Columbia, Fort McLeod, in 1805. The Nor'westers were expecting big things from the fur trade in this new territory, which they called New Caledonia. But first they needed to find a navigable canoe route down to the Pacific Ocean from the interior. Such a route would enable them to carry their furs to the coast for shipment to market, and to carry supplies back to the trading posts. It was in search of this route that Simon Fraser's expedition set off down the river in May 1808.

"We had to pass where no human being should venture." These words were part of Fraser's own description of his harrowing trip. They are words that capture the combination of daring and danger that marked the expedition. They also reflect his deep disappointment that, in the end, the route he pioneered was too wild to be of any use to the fur traders. The rapids were too long; the portages were too steep; the danger was too great. Twenty years later the fur trade governor George Simpson canoed the same route and concluded: "I should consider the passage down to be certain Death, in nine attempts out of ten."

As the title of her book suggests, Campbell's subject is the river as much as it is Simon Fraser. The Fraser is British

Columbia's longest and most important waterway. Winding 1,400 kilometres from high up in the Rocky Mountains down to the Pacific Ocean at Vancouver, it drains about one quarter of the province. Nowadays, 65 per cent of all the people living in British Columbia live in its watershed. In Simon Fraser's time, the river was valued for the rich stocks of salmon that provided food for the First Nations people whose villages dotted its banks. No longer as wild and untamed as it was, the river is still prone to serious flooding in the spring, and its roughest parts are still impossible for boats to navigate.

The Savage River is a novel. It should not be read as an exact account of Simon Fraser's expedition. Campbell used her imagination to recreate what she believed may have happened. But she was fortunate in having Fraser's journal of the trip in which he recorded what occurred in great detail. Campbell follows the journal closely; in a way her book is a dramatization of Fraser's own words.

When it was first published, thirty-five years ago, *The Savage River* was intended to answer the complaint that Canada's young people did not know as much as they should about the history of their country. It is appropriate that Marjorie Wilkins Campbell's book should come back into print at the beginning of a new century, when once again we hear the same complaint being voiced. In fact, there is always a need to tell Canadians, young and old, about the men and women who came before. Their stories never go out of fashion. They are the stories of our country.

Daniel Francis, *Author and Historian*

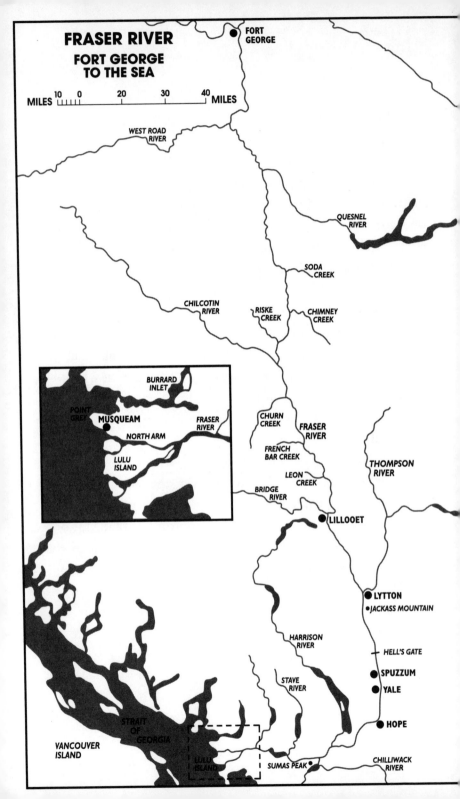

FRASER RIVER
FORT GEORGE TO THE SEA

MILES 10 0 20 30 40 MILES

FORT GEORGE

WEST ROAD RIVER

QUESNEL RIVER

SODA CREEK

CHILCOTIN RIVER

RISKE CREEK

CHIMNEY CREEK

BURRARD INLET

POINT GREY

MUSQUEAM

FRASER RIVER

NORTH ARM

LULU ISLAND

CHURN CREEK

FRASER RIVER

FRENCH BAR CREEK

LEON CREEK

THOMPSON RIVER

BRIDGE RIVER

LILLOOET

LYTTON

JACKASS MOUNTAIN

HARRISON RIVER

HELL'S GATE

SPUZZUM

YALE

STAVE RIVER

STRAIT OF GEORGIA

HOPE

VANCOUVER ISLAND

LULU ISLAND

CHILLIWACK RIVER

SUMAS PEAK

One
The Date with Destiny

*What mattered now above all else was the search
for a route that would reduce the enormous cost of the long
canoe-haul from Montreal. On this the future of the
North West Company depended.*

*S*imon Fraser stepped outside early to see what the morning promised. A fine day, he hoped. Good weather always helped a canoe trip, especially on the first day out. But fair weather or foul, nothing would delay his departure now. Today was the day he had thought about and planned for more than three years.

For a moment he stood brooding before the open door of the log cabin, a strong, determined-looking man with a thatch of reddish hair unkempt from sleeping. No use trying to see through the fog that still obscured the spruce on the far bank and most of the strong-flowing river. In the pre-dawn the fog was so thick and cold and damp that it penetrated his woollen coat and corduroy trousers and heavy moccasins. But while he had to beat his arms against his body to get his circulation going, his years of life in the open told him what he wanted to know: by noon, if the sun came out—and he thought it would—the day would be hot. That was a good omen.

No man accustomed to the outdoors—certainly not one with the blood of a Highland Scot—could suppress a surge of excitement on such a morning; it lay like gold on his stomach, as his mother used to say. Soon, when the men were loading the canoes, he would feel quiet again. For this private moment he faced the trip with mingled hope and fear and a fervent unspoken prayer.

Ever since his sixteenth birthday he had spent most of his

summers on canoe trips, and he was now past thirty. In other years he had travelled hundreds, sometimes thousands, of miles in a birch-bark canoe from spring until freeze-up. Never had there been a trip like this. Always before he had known that some other white man had travelled the river before him. He had known, more or less, how far the journey would be, how long it would take, how much dried provisions would be needed.

"Good morning to you, Mr. Fraser!"

Fraser dropped his tensed arms at the greeting from his friend and lieutenant, John Stuart, and the new clerk, Jules Quesnel.

"Good morning to you, gentlemen!"

Stuart, only a few years younger than he, had been with him for three fur-trading seasons on the Upper Peace and in the territory on the Pacific slope of the Rocky Mountains that Fraser had named New Caledonia. Quesnel, aged twenty-two, was one of the two clerks who last autumn had brought west the trade goods that made the present trip possible. He was to be third in command.

As Fraser spoke to his aides the little patch of clearing on the riverside in front of Fort George sprang into activity. Voyageurs tumbled out of their tents or the new, raw-looking log shacks in which they had slept.

"*Bonjour, mon bourgeois!*"

Hardly pausing to greet him, they swore at one another in early morning camaraderie. All spoke the patois of French and Indian that they had picked up along thousands of miles of rivers and from a score of Indian tribes, with an occasional word of English accented by a rich Scottish burr. Only the two local

Indians who were to go on the trip as guides and interpreters were silent. There was no pause for breakfast. That would come later along the way, at nine o'clock perhaps, or at eleven.

The noisy talk lasted only briefly, and there was no horse-play; Fraser would not tolerate that. Though he was respected for his fairness, every voyageur knew he would not hesitate to flog a man who disobeyed an order without very good reason or whose conduct threatened the safety of the expedition or the supplies they had paddled and portaged at great cost across the continent. The story of the voyageur who tried to keep an Indian girl against Company rules had been retold at many an evening camp-fire.

The *bourgeois* had sent her away, the voyageurs recounted. Then he had taken his gun from him, his blanket, his axe, his dog, and his bow and arrow. When the man still refused to give up the girl, he was literally kicked out of the trading-post: "And dat girl, I think maybe she like her man more, maybe . . ."

The story was matched by another about a voyageur who was fined his entire year's pay for carelessly neglecting to secure a loaded canoe. In the early nineteenth century such stern discipline was as common in the fur trade as in the army and navy.

Yet every one of the nineteen French-Canadian voyageurs who were to accompany him on the trip wanted to go, and not because his contract required it. That Fraser knew. They might argue and fight among themselves, especially over a Métis girl. But they were born to this life, though most cared little about exploration. As boys along the St. Lawrence they had watched their fathers and older brothers leave Montreal for the *pays d'en haut*, longing for the year when they would be old enough to follow. They were northmen who had paddled thousands of miles without losing one per cent of the Company's goods.

It was a voyageur's proud boast that he could carry two ninety-pound packs or more over a portage. He might even carry a canoe. He competed with his fellows to see who could paddle longest against a strong current without stopping for a "pipe." He liked to gauge his popularity as much by the range and colour of his profanity as by his courage. And, as Fraser realized only too fully, they would need all their vaunted prowess before this trip ended. Any one of them, or the entire party, might be swirled to his death in a raging whirlpool if the river proved to be as bad as the Indians said it was. But for the fact that Alexander Mackenzie (like Fraser a partner in the North West Company) had recently made that gruelling trip which proved a man could reach the Pacific Ocean overland, they might be going to the moon. In all the known world few trips promised greater challenge or higher adventure.

It was always the same when they were leaving on a long trip; everything seemed to happen at once. Voyageurs scurried from the warehouse, bent low as they shouldered packs and kegs down to the waterside where the canoes floated. Others gently steadied the canoes as poles were laid on the thwarts to support the assembled cargo. It all seemed so simple and easy and smooth; actually, the apparent ease of loading a canoe resulted from superb planning and wide experience and considerable practical imagination.

Even the log fort beside this almost unknown river was part of a gigantic plan. For three years Fraser had been exploring the streams flowing into the Upper Peace, searching for water routes that might lead to the Pacific. He had built one forward base after another, encouraging the Indians to trap furs and exchange them for kettles or knives or beads or a taste of rum, always with a twofold purpose, trade and exploration. Furs were the North West Company's lucrative business, and Canada's first major industry. The business depended on finding new sources of furs and on locating the new streams along which the trade would move. Fraser, like every other fur trader–explorer, had to rely on one Indian band after another for information and food.

Fort George, the newest in a string of isolated posts stretching thousands of miles back to Montreal, was only a group of log shacks, each with a crude stone fireplace and beds made of poles and bark, all surrounded by a strong, rough stockade of pointed logs. There was nothing else, except for the four canoes floating on the freshet-swollen river that still did not have a name.

The canoes, unlike the fort, were not all new, a fact that caused Fraser much concern. Stuart, the only experienced canoe-builder in the vast area, was primarily a fur trader. He could spare little time to build new canoes. There were too few voyageurs to search for suitable bark and pine gum or to pull cedar roots for *wattap*, the strong thread that held the pieces of bark together. Already the season was late, and no more trade goods could be got from the depot at Fort William, two thousand miles east. Dependent on his own resources, Fraser had good reason for naming his own old canoe, his flagship, *Perseverance*. That word was the motto of the company in which he had been a partner for eight years.

The canoes were designed for swift rivers, and light enough to be carried by two men. Each held a ton of trade goods, plus five or six men and their personal gear and food. In a letter to Stuart during the winter, Fraser had painstakingly calculated the cargo to the last pound, including all the goods he had saved out of the past two years' supplies: " . . . 10 pieces [of] goods exclusive of Provisions will answer for going below viz. 3 Bales [of cotton goods] $^1/_2$ Bale Kettles, $^1/_2$ Case Guns 1 Cassette 1 Case Iron $^1/_2$ Rolls Tobacco, 1 Keg Powder, 1 Bag Ball, 1 Bag shot, and $^1/_2$ Keg high wines & I doubt if this same can be spared."

The clerks had been given carefully prepared lists of the items that were to go into each canoe, and the voyageurs did the loading while Fraser supervised the entire project, not daring to risk leaving a single essential pack behind. Everything had to go into place so that each craft would be properly balanced. Balance, the guides insisted, was so important that it mattered on which side a man wore the feather in his cap.

Years of travelling in small canoes had limited each man's personal outfit to a bare minimum which could be stowed in a tight roll under the seats—a couple of blankets, a change of buckskin shirt and breeches, a coloured sash or *ceinture fléchée* for rare dress-up occasions, and extra moccasins because jagged rock often shredded a pair in a day's portaging. The treasures that really mattered to every voyageur were his own paddle, his hunting knife, and his *sac à feu* in which he kept his precious tobacco and pipe. Because of their rank the clerks were entitled to a pound or so of tea and chocolate, which probably would not last for more than a few suppers.

Fraser did not mind what the men took along, providing the

packs did not exceed the prescribed weight and size. He was more concerned about the supply of dried salmon, the staple provision on the Pacific slope, the rolls of birch bark for repairing rents in the canoes, and the kegs of gum and bundles of *wattap* for sealing the rents. The expedition must also have strong tow-lines and extra paddles, a first-aid kit and medicines. He found a special place for his tiny tent, for his writing case, and for the paper and quills and ink that he and Stuart would need; Stuart was to write the official log. Right at hand were the compasses and the sextant on which they would base the record of the trip. Finally, into the *Perseverance* Fraser's guide carefully stowed the most important item of the entire cargo, his notes.

They made a slim packet, those notes meticulously copied from the reports of men who had some knowledge of the Pacific coast—Spaniards and Russians, Captain Vancouver and the American Captain Gray who had sailed into the mouth of the river believed to be the Columbia, Alexander Mackenzie, and a few others. But Simon Fraser had with him practically all the information known to men whose eyes were on the Pacific; it had been garnered by his partners on trips to London and New York and Boston, and sent on hopefully. There was nothing more to add to the cargo, except the pieces of yellow oilcloth, or crocus, faded from exposure to sun and wind and water. When tied over the carefully stowed cargo they were adequate protection against any average storm.

No one thought about sending farewell messages. The last canoes that could get messages to Montreal within a year had already left.

Everything was ready. Stuart, Quesnel, and a senior guide waited in their places in their respective canoes, which rode so low that the water lapped the gunwales. Fraser shook hands with Hugh Faries, the clerk who had come west with Quesnel and who would remain in charge of the fort. Then, with the bowman steadying the *Perseverance*, he eased himself onto his narrow seat and grasped a paddle; on this expedition every man would work.

The fog had lifted slightly, improving visibility. This well-treed country, low except for the high north bank of the Nechako River coming in from the west, might be a stretch of the familiar terrain east of the Rockies but for one significant fact: the river on which they were embarked did not flow to the east; it flowed south and, please God, westward.

Fraser looked at his chronometer. Five o'clock.

The nineteen voyageurs waited tensely in their places, cold hands gripping their paddles, longing for the order that would start them on their way and the warmth that would come with exercise.

"*Bon voyage!*" cried Faries, and Fraser spoke the single word that got the tiny expedition under way.

"*Allez!*"

Twenty-four paddles dug into the swift, muddy stream in fine, strong rhythm.

"Having made every necessary preparation for a long voyage . . .," the party left Fort George on Saturday morning, May 8, 1808, determined to follow the river to the sea. Fraser hoped he was on the Columbia, the only river known from coastal explorations that seemed likely to be navigable. So desperately did the Nor'Westers need such a river that, in his letters of instruction to his clerks, he had already referred to the stream on which they were embarked as the Columbia. With a navigable link between New Caledonia and the Pacific the Company could economically send down furs from the western posts and bring up trade goods shipped around the Horn. It might even develop an extensive trade with the Orient, though that was a secondary hope. What mattered now above all else was the search for a route that would reduce the enormous cost of the long canoe-haul from Montreal. On this the future of the North West Company depended.

Two
Crocus and Charcoal

*But as he squatted beside the . . . Indian and watched him
draw his crude impressions with the charcoal end of a stick,
one fact became very clear: If the man was right,
this river was the worst he had ever travelled.*

*A*t eleven Fraser ordered the stop for breakfast. For an hour he had been looking for a good place to land without having to unload the canoes and with enough space for camps for himself, the clerks, and the men.

The men scrambled up the bank, chattering noisily, flexing muscles cramped from six hours' paddling, and ravenously hungry. Their disciplined decorum nearly broke as they waited, hunting knives ready, for the clerks to hand out their rations. Then, as if the scene had been rehearsed hundreds of times on this stretch of river bank, every buckskin-clad voyageur squatted on the nearest fallen timber. The noisy chatter stopped. Not a word was spoken as they hacked and chewed or broke off tasty bits with their fingers. Today, and on every day when provisions were plentiful, they would eat two big meals. When supplies ran low, it would be three, not nearly so bountiful; on three meals a day, Fraser had observed, a man did the maximum paddling and carrying on the minimum amount of salmon. Day after day, with very few exceptions, the diet would be dried salmon. There might even be days when a man's belly craved more of it.

After the meal, while the men rested briefly, Fraser made the notes on which he hoped to base his report of the expedition. Stuart carefully removed his sextant and astronomical tables from the cork-lined box, and took a "meridian altitude, O.L.L. 115°9′45″ by artificial Horizon. Error of Sextant 7′30″+." There being no large or other smooth water surface in the area suitable for a natural horizon, he determined their latitude with the aid of one of the mercury mirrors that had come into general use during the past decade. Meantime Quesnel checked each canoe for necessary repairs.

By one o'clock every man was back in his place, refreshed, paddling strongly with a swift-flowing current. This was one of the comparatively rare occasions that made a voyageur's life worth living. Always alert, wet paddles flashing as the high clay banks rushed by, each was ready when the steersman sang a few tentative words from a familiar song. Soon all sang, except the Indians. They marvelled at these strange sounds that for them had no significance! What was *à la claire fontaine*? Or *la rose blanche*? Fraser only half listened to the nostalgic chansons. He was watching the shoreline and the rippling current, wondering whether the footprint of a red deer he had seen at the noon stop meant that there was plenty of game in the area. The rough structures he saw here and there were, he knew, summer fishing-shelters used by Indians during salmon runs. Late in the afternoon two specially large shelters near the inflow of a river from the west attracted his attention, and the canoes were briefly beached.

This was the West Road River, "80 yards wide," up which Alexander Mackenzie had travelled fifteen years earlier, before trudging overland on his way to Bella Coola. Fraser called it *Bourbonneur*. Intending to follow his river to the sea, he was only casually interested. But he took a good look at the Indian dwellings, and left gifts to assure the absent owners that he came as a friend. At six o'clock, a few miles beyond the West Road River, he called the stop for the night. They had travelled sixty miles in thirteen hours. It was a very good beginning.

Two camps were made, Fraser maintaining the early-nineteenth-century discipline that separated the "gentlemen" from the men, and everyone got to work. Some of the voyageurs gathered wood for the fires. Others pulled wild onions to flavour the dried salmon stew that soon smelled so tantalizing that no one could wait until the onions were cooked.

Before dark, Fraser crawled into his tent and opened his portable writing-desk. "Put our arms in order, gave ammunition to all hands and established a regular watch," he wrote before he fell asleep. He had been in unknown, probably dangerous, country often before, and he had taken every possible precaution, but he also had to get some sleep. In a few hours he would take his turn at sentry duty.

The morning dawned so bitterly cold that he made a note of it while the men still slept, each rolled in his blanket on the ground with only the upturned canoes for protection against the wind and river fog.

"*Lève! Lève!*"

The men needed minutes to stretch their numbed bodies and to rub the lingering sleep from their eyes. Mechanically, each rolled his blanket. Everyone was in his place by four o'clock.

Two hours later the little brigade reached the rapids at Cottonwood Canyon. After shouldering eighty ninety-pound packs over a very rough trail and tracking the canoes down white water, no one remembered that he had so recently been numb with cold. Below the canyon, Fraser cached three bales of salmon, partly to reduce the loads, partly to assure the men that there would be provisions for the return trip. As they would do at every cache, the men collected driftwood timbers and from them built strong hangars. On these well-marked scaffolds the bales were secured, out of reach of marauding animals and protected by boughs from sun, wind, and rain.

Fraser hoped to barter for food along the way, using articles from his packs of assorted trade goods as currency. But the Montreal fur traders had been able to explore their way across the continent in a few decades only because they had set up strategic caches of easily procured native foods to provision their brigades; so great were the distances they had to travel in each comparatively short summer season that there could be little time for hunting or fishing along the way.

Until recently pemmican had been the sole staple for the *pays d'en haut*; Fraser had eaten little else except this dried, pounded buffalo meat since he was sixteen. Good or bad, a hungry man soon got to like it, and could paddle all day on two or three pounds. Pemmican also carried easily in ninety-pound buffalo-hide sacks that could be stowed in a canoe, and it kept well in all sorts of weather.

With no buffalo, or pemmican, available on the Pacific slope, Fraser had added a second staple during the three years he had been establishing New Caledonia. The West Coast Indians relied on salmon, fresh or dried. So did he. Sometimes the scene after a good salmon run reminded him of a buffalo hunt. The routine was much the same. After the men had speared or netted their catch, women took over the stinking, messy chore of cleaning and preparing the food for smoking. After the inevitable carnage of killing, nothing could be more pleasant or appetizing than the fragrant smell of buffalo meat or strings of salmon hanging on racks to dry over embers or in the sun. In the spring of 1808 much of the success of Fraser's expedition depended on bales of salmon, as dry as sticks of wood, tied tight with spruce-bark cord. A good supply would save men from starving to death, a tragedy that had happened more than once across the continent before adequate food caches were established.

Shortly before sunset the four canoes passed another fairly large river flowing in from the east. This Fraser named for his young clerk, Jules Quesnel. Then the expedition camped for the second night, seventeen hours after the "*Lève! Lève!*" Perhaps because the men were not yet settled into a team, or because they had spent so long building the salmon cache or battling white water, today the run was only half that of the first day, about thirty miles.

Fraser was not discouraged by the reduced mileage. Indeed, in a brief, neatly written journal entry, he found himself questioning the Indians' warnings that the river was so bad: "The country all along is charming . . . interspersed with meadows and hills, dales & high rocks, [it] has upon the whole a *romantic* but *pleasant* appearance." Game obviously was plentiful. He had also seen so many fishing-shelters that he knew the country was well inhabited.

Had he been a man with less practical experience as a North American trader-explorer, Fraser might have paid less attention to the natives' rough summer dwellings and to the people who inhabited them. But the sixteen years in which he had risen from clerk to full partner in charge of one of the most important trading areas in the uncharted north-west third of the continent had taught him to depend on tried aboriginal customs and on the people who had evolved those customs. The lesson was part of the tradition he and his partners had inherited from the French.

From the Indians the white men had learned the use of the canoe and the snowshoe and the tump-line by which they carried their packs on their shoulders. They also learned to depend on contact with previously unknown Indians, since each band or tribe naturally knew its neighbours and whether they were likely to be friendly or hostile. Pausing to greet bands along the river delayed progress. It also made progress possible.

"Who are they?"

Fraser directed his interpreter's attention to a small group of Indians on the left bank. They had the first horses he had seen on the Pacific slope. "Steer for the right bank," he ordered.

Before the canoes could be hauled out of the water, another group of Indians suddenly rushed out of the bushes, gripping their bows and arrows with unmistakable intent. Fraser and his clerks whipped out their pistols and covered the landing. Then, each party glowering at the other and the Indians yelling in a strange dialect at both the newcomers and those on the far bank, Simon Fraser told his interpreter to try to explain who he was and that his mission was peaceful.

For tense minutes he covered the chief of the threatening band while the interpreter alternately tried loud words and silent sign language; though he and his men were well armed, they had their backs to the swift-flowing river and were in a bad position to defend themselves. Gradually, his unflinching attitude and the interpreter's efforts eased the tension. These Indians were a party of Atnah from the west, trying to communicate with the horsemen across the river. Fraser stepped forward to shake hands, and the Atnah chief put down his bow. Soon white men and Indians exchanged their defensive attitude for friendly communication, the Atnah chief proudly relaying everything he learned about the white men to the Indians across the water, including the news that they were going to the ocean. Fraser knew he had met up with not one but two friendly bands. He could safely cross over to talk to the horsemen.

When he had shaken hands with the chief of the Tauten, he met a youth who could speak with his own interpreter, and communication soon became comparatively easy, much to Fraser's relief. Not only did the Tauten have horses, but they were so well armed that they were obviously better potential friends than foes.

After the usual formalities the explorer admired the Tauten's weapons and complimented the chief on the excellent construction of the bows and arrows. Each bow was made of cedar and juniper and was covered with the skins of rattlesnakes which, he was told, were common to the area. The arrows were tipped with stone as hard as flint. The Tauten's leather clothes and shoes and their fine buckskin, caribou, and beaver robes assured the fur trader that there must be plenty of rich fur-bearing animals in the area. But furs were not the main object of this trip: Had any of the Tauten been to the ocean? he asked. Did they know of anyone who had travelled so far?

Though none had been to the ocean, continued questioning revealed a man who had guided Alexander Mackenzie. He had little useful information, either about Mackenzie or about the nature of the river. Like practically every Indian Fraser had talked with, Mackenzie's guide advised going overland with horses to carry men and packs.

Perhaps the Indians were right. But Fraser wondered if they might also be telling him what they thought he wanted to hear. Fraser decided to try to make clear to them that he really wanted true information about the river and that he was powerful enough to get what he wanted. He decided that an exhibition of the effectiveness of his weapons might produce the best results.

The Tauten had heard of fire-arms, but had never seen any. Warning them all to stand well back, he and his clerks fired their pistols into the air. The Indians dropped to the ground in terror. When they were persuaded to come close again, Fraser showed them the marks of the explosives on a tree. He then had one of the guns fired, during which a cracked swivel was shattered by the blast. Fortunately, no one was injured except the gunner, whose wound was superficial. But the close escape provided a good lesson for the clerks about the careful use of their weapons: the death or serious injury of a single Indian would have made the entire Pacific slope unsafe for every white man. Fraser turned the near-accident to good account by letting the natives watch while he dressed the gunner's wound, and assured them that the wound would heal. Dressing the wound—or firing the gun—so impressed one Indian that he told Fraser about a chief farther down the river who had a slave who had been to the sea.

This was the news Fraser wanted to hear. It brightened the third day of the journey even more than the fact that the expedition had that day travelled fifty miles.

In the morning, while the voyageurs were carrying packs

over the tortuous trail at the Soda Creek Canyon rapids and tracking the canoes, he went to see the chief who had a slave who had been to the ocean.

Fraser smoked with the chief and his leading men at their camp on a hill overlooking the river. He held in his hands a calumet said to have come from near the Pacific. He accepted a fine deerskin and a prime beaver pelt, ate excellent dried salmon, and pretended to enjoy some unappetizing roots obviously relished by his hosts. In return he gave them a little tobacco, which they greatly preferred to their own blend of dried leaves and grease. Again the calumet was passed and Fraser talked about establishing trading-posts along the river. When he could not bear to wait another minute, he asked about the slave.

The slave talked much and said little that was significant.

"Bring me a couple of crocus!" Fraser ordered.

The weathered yellow oilcloths were laid on the ground. Taking a piece of charcoal from the fire, Fraser asked the slave to draw a sketch of the river.

How often had he and other explorers asked an Indian to make one of those rough maps of a North American river? Fraser himself had had many sketches marked out on river sand with a stick. He hoped the piece of oilcloth would make possible something more exact. Perhaps it did. He could not know for certain. But as he squatted beside the slave Indian and watched him draw his crude impressions with the charcoal end of a stick, one fact became very clear: If the man was right, this river was the worst he had ever travelled. It might not even be navigable all the way if the comments of the natives standing about the two men bent over the crocus could be relied on; the chief warned Fraser that he would have to abandon the canoes, cache the packs, and travel overland.

Simon Fraser sat back on his moccasin heels and looked about him—at the group of Indians, at his own men, at the swift, unknown river swirling below the eroded claybank—and said he would go on as planned.

The Tauten chief's eyes shone with admiration. For a moment, as Fraser rose to his feet, the two men stood appraising one another. Then the Indian spoke: If Fraser was determined to go, he would go too, to guide him, and he would take with them the slave who said he had been to the sea. Fraser eagerly accepted the offer—it was better luck than he had dared hope for. He suspected that what the chief really wanted was a promise to erect the next new trading-post in the area. Before setting out again, he cached four more bales of salmon, entrusting them to the personal care of the chief's brother.

A strong south wind hampered the progress of the little brigade, now increased to five canoes, when Fraser resumed his journey late in the afternoon. Almost immediately the character of the river banks changed. Great rocks jutted through the clay. Rocks kept the canoemen out in the wind-tossed middle stream where the combination of south wind and strong, south-flowing river threatened momentarily to swing them out of control. When the ominous roar of a rapids rose above the wind's moan, Fraser signalled a halt short of Chimney Creek Canyon, much to the relief of every man in his party. He was thankful when the Tauten chief indicated a comparatively safe landing-place where the canoes were quickly beached.

With the old chief and his guides, Fraser went ahead to

inspect the mile or so of white water and dark, swirling whirlpools. Surely, he suggested, the Indians did not attempt to run that stretch of the river?

The old man's reply touched him, while it warned him that he must also evaluate his advice. No, said the Tauten chief, the Indians would never run those rapids, but his confidence in the superiority of the white men was so great that, if Fraser suggested it, they would do so!

The decision depended on Fraser alone.

He surveyed the white water rushing between high rock and clay banks. His men were experts at running white water. But his canoes were old and had been often mended. Because it was now too late in the day to make either a portage or a *décharge* before dark, he postponed the decision until the morning. In the morning his men would be rested and better able to handle the difficult situation.

Back at his camp, Fraser had the Tauten chief's bed made up in his own tent, in case he should change his mind about going on; if the chief backed out, so, also, would the slave. But the Indian showed every indication that the white man had won his entire respect. He even suggested that Fraser get his pistols and guns ready: Most Indians were good people, he said, but there might be some who would creep about in the dark, bent on plunder or worse. Fraser had already taken that precaution.

That night, sharing his narrow tent with his guide, he hoped the river would not be as bad as the charcoal sketch on the crocus had suggested. Ahead lay the worst stretch so far, and that day they had travelled only twenty miles, a third as far as on the first day.

Three

You Can't Get Out of the Canyon

*The worst part of the canyon, the part through which
the river raged white for most of the way, was probably less
than two miles long. But what appallingly difficult miles!*

*F*ortunately, Fraser could not know how long it would take to clear the Chimney Creek rapids.

As soon as the early morning fog lifted, he returned to inspect the situation, accompanied by Stuart and six of the men. The worst part of the canyon, the part through which the river raged white for most of the way, was probably less than two miles long. But what appallingly difficult miles! In places the gut narrowed to thirty or forty yards in width, and through that narrow space rushed the entire body of water, piling up on itself in a succession of sickeningly deep whirlpools. Overnight, Fraser estimated, melting snows in the mountains had raised the river's general level by at least eight feet, greatly increasing its volume and their peril.

The white men, accompanied by a number of Tauten and Atnah Indians, could not make themselves heard above the roar of the torrent. But there was no need to shout at one another. A long, concerted look at the tortuous trails up the high hills over which they would have to carry canoes and packs turned their eyes back to the river. Of the two evils, the savage river seemed the lesser.

Fraser had yet another danger to face, one that troubled each of the white men: the Indians. They seemed friendly. They had been helpful and co-operative. But he dared not trust them completely, not when the loaded canoes had to pass under those high, rocky banks where it would be in their power to sink every one of them.

He stationed Stuart and two voyageurs at the lower end of the rapid to guard the down-going canoes, and returned to the upper end to send off the first. Lightened to a dozen pieces and manned by five of the ablest canoemen, it shot out into the current at a terrifying speed, into the whirlpool at the nearest cascade. For half a second, as Fraser watched, the whirlpool held it motionless, before releasing it to spin like a chip. Then for minutes it whirled out of control until another current or the sheer skill and desperation of the men got it back into safer water. But not into safety. Still like a chip, it continued in the power of the river, leaping from one crest to another until the second, and last, terrible cascade forced it out of the water, onto a rock that chanced to provide a low, comparatively safe landing.

Never, in all the treacherous water they had travelled from the St. Lawrence, by way of the Ottawa, the Saskatchewan, and the Peace, had his voyageurs risked white water worse than this. To attempt to run the rest of the rapids would be sheer suicide.

Racing along the high, rough trail Fraser met Stuart who had also watched helplessly while the men paddled for their lives. Together, the two stumbled down the slippery, precipitous bank, plunging their daggers into the clay and rock to check their speed and to save themselves from sliding into the river. The voyageurs were all alive. They could climb out of the canyon by the same means as Fraser and Stuart had eased themselves down. Hoisting the canoe up to the hills that had seemed impassable and carrying the packs promised to be far more dangerous.

Again due to a combination of fate and the superb skill of the men, most of the cargo was still intact. When it was removed, Fraser had a stout line tied to the bow of the canoe.

Meanwhile, several men laboriously hacked steps out of the long, rocky bank, each no more than a foot wide. Then began a slow, hazardous haul and carry during which a false step by any one of them would have hurled them all into the river along with the birch-bark craft.

By the time the baggage had been hauled or hoisted up the bank, night came on. The river had forced Fraser to change his plans and to portage both canoes and packs.

In the morning, he was glad to accept the Tauten chief's offer of men and four horses and the assistance of several Atnah to help carry the pack and the canoes; somehow he and the two clerks would manage to keep a surreptitious guard over the straggling, much-needed natives. Before the day was over he knew they were by no means his worst threat. That continued to come from the river itself, and from its treacherous banks. The horse carrying Stuart's writing-case and part of the first-aid supplies lost its footing and fell into the river. With it went the precious supplies. None were retrieved. The incident almost broke the morale of some of the voyageurs, as did another rough sketch of the river, equally as sobering as the first.

"I imagine they have not got the better of the fright they had running down the rapids yesterday," observed the explorer in the privacy of his journal, "but notwithstanding we shall try it tomorrow."

He was overly optimistic. They were three entire exhausting days at the portage, during which the Tauten chief repeatedly advised him to abandon the canoes and to travel by horse overland. By the overland route he would come eventually to another stream flowing into this bad river, one where white men were said to be—"Whether it had been Capt. Lewis or some of the Fort des Prairie[s] people we cannot determine," Fraser observed. Not even the vague hope of seeing the American Captain Meriwether Lewis or Fraser's own friend David Thompson swayed him: "Going to the sea by an indirect way was not the object of the undertaking."

But steadily the river forced him to modify all hopes of running the Chimney Creek rapids under present conditions. These appalling conditions were partly due, he thought, to the sudden melting of snows in the mountains, a situation that might improve when the volume of water in the narrow gut dropped, perhaps on their return journey. Now, caught between the steep rocks of the canyon, it could swamp a canoe with its contents and every man on board in seconds.

A clear, swift run brought the expedition to yet more rapids and a long portage more hazardous than the last because loose stones and gravel covered the high, narrow trail. His alert eyes watching every operation, Fraser suddenly saw a voyageur poised on a rocky ledge, unable to go forward or back, unable to unload his pack without himself following it down into the river.

Hurrying to the man's relief, Fraser knew he must not risk a single unsure step: on his life depended not only that of the desperate fellow on the precipice but of the entire expedition. Clawing his way along the rock he had decided what he must do by the time he reached the ledge. A single, sure swipe with his hunting-knife cut loose the pack. As he steadied the sweating voyageur, they both silently watched the pack plummet into the river, and more precious supplies disappear beyond recovery.

That night, like every other man in the party, Fraser suffered agonies from cut and blistered feet; practically every moccasin had been torn by the sharp rocks.

He had scant time or opportunity for smelling wild sagebrush or roses, or observing shrubs that in a month or two would yield quantities of luscious small fruits. Only in passing did he realize that the country was swiftly changing to flat, arid highlands carpeted with grass that could maintain big game and many people. Every mile the current flowed faster. Every mile the banks soared higher and more menacing. Occasionally the small brigade made excellent time, especially in good weather and as the water level dropped. Increasingly often they were forced to portage. At the place known today as Iron Rapids, between Riske Creek and the inflow of the Chilcotin River, packs and canoes had to be carried for a mile. It was so unbelievably bad that Fraser made a note in his journal, in case he might not later trust his memory.

"The river here, which does not exceed thirty yards in breadth, passes between two precipices, and is turbulent, noisy, and awful to behold! . . . the men took five horses to transport the baggage across, yet were much harrassed with fatigue."

Hauling the canoes up and down the rocky defiles was so much more dangerous and fatiguing then carrying the packs that he added a further note: "Incredible it is to relate the trouble and misery the people had in performing that office." Hoping that nowhere could the river be worse than here, he tapped the small keg of rum and gave every man a dram. It was all the rum he had. But it might hearten them to continue, and they would have one less burden to carry. To make an occasion of overcoming the worst hazard so far, he named the place *Portage du Baril*.

Again they had an exciting run, only slightly handicapped by driftwood, shooting rapid after rapid, each so swift there was no time to look about. Every eye and muscle alert, the men in their frail canoes raced around sharp bends between nearly perpendicular banks with little possibility of stopping and nowhere to land. When Fraser later recorded the terror of those swings around each successive acute bend, he did so in the terse words of a physically exhausted man: "Had we suddenly come upon a cascade or bad Rapid, . . . it is more than likely that all of us would have perished, which is much to be apprehended."

And ahead, warned the Tauten chief, the river was really impassable. No canoes could get through the *Rapide Couvert*.

Fraser and his clerks almost agreed when they looked at this latest obstacle, and Fraser sent Quesnel to search for a suitable portage. Three hours later the young clerk returned: there was a trail, about four miles long, through wild country across the river. Without the sobering experience of the past few days Fraser might have tried it without further investigation. But now they were almost into the mountains and he did not know what added hazard to expect.

All day the mountains had been visible to the right, ever since the morning sun brightened their snowcapped peaks. For miles they had seemed far away. Now, as the men came up from the river to survey the scene, they appeared to be much closer and straight ahead. The Indians said the river cut through them.

Fraser talked it over with the old chief, his clerks, and the guides. The river level had dropped a couple of feet, and might quickly drop lower.

"As it is my object to determine the practicability of the navigation of this River, tho' it would be much more safe and expeditious to go by land, we shall not leave our canoes as long as there will be any possibility of taking them down by water or land." To be sure they could go on by canoe, he prudently ordered Stuart and Quesnel, with the chief, the interpreter, and several voyageurs, to survey the situation in the morning.

Fraser did not go with them.

Earlier in the day he had hurt himself, how seriously he did not yet know. Struggling along the side of a steep bank with nothing to get hold of, he had strained himself so severely that he now suffered violent pain in his groin. The pain was so acute that he could hardly walk a step.

He had seen other men in agony from hernias caused by overstrain. A bad rupture put a man in a desperate situation. It could prevent him from travelling at all or incapacitate him so seriously that, in the case of a voyageur, he might have to be left behind with food and a man to stay with him, if a man could be spared. Fraser was not a voyageur. He was the leader of a costly expedition on which the future of his company might depend, and the lives of the men with him. He was too heavy to be carried on a litter, if a litter could be carried along this river. He could only hope that a few hours' rest might ease his pain.

He spent the next two days in camp; while the clerks were absent there was plenty for the remaining voyageurs to do, repairing canoes and moccasins which here never lasted more than a few days. He had the salmon counted and sorted; due to very hot weather some of it had already spoiled. Only 2,500 fish remained, barely enough for a month, and though he hoped to get more by trading with the Indians downstream, he dared not count on this in the mountains ahead which were, according to the Indians, very high and covered with snow, the highest on the entire river.

The clerks returned from their reconnaissance trip on the afternoon of the third day, without the chief and the interpreter; they had remained downstream with another band of Indians. Stuart tried to describe the awful *Rapide Couvert* to Fraser. He found the task beyond his "slender abilities even was I possessed of more leisure and materials than I am." But despite its terrible hazards he thought the rapid could be run more readily than the canoes could be carried over hills which were higher and more precipitous than at Chimney Creek Canyon.

Stuart also described the Indians they had met below the rapids, with whom the Tauten chief and the interpreter had stayed, a band of apparently friendly Lillooet. Knowing he would have to depend on these Lillooet, and well aware of the advantage of making a good impression on strange Indians, Fraser had his men put on their best shirts before breaking camp. He gave each of the two interpreters from Fort George a blanket and breeches, so that "they may appear decent and Englishified among strangers"; they had been clothed only in deerskin and beaver. At seven in the morning the party was ready to leave, "our arms and every thing being in due order."

It was a fearsome sight, the *Rapide Couvert*. The channel, Fraser estimated, contracted to forty yards, with banks so precipitous a man could hardly see to the top; the left was upwards of 1,200 feet high. Both banks had been so undercut by the river that they were narrower above than at the water level. Between them the river lashed itself into great waves. It was, he thought, as he had already thought several times before, "the most dangerous place we hitherto passed."

Four canoes were put into the rapids without any packs; the *Perseverance* carried a token cargo and six voyageurs. "All hands without hesitation embarked, as it were a *corp perdu* upon the mercy of this Stygian tide. Once embarked the die was cast, and the great difficulty consisted in keeping the canoes in the medium, or *fil d'eau*, that is to say, clear of the precipice on one side, and of the gulphs formed by the waves on the other. However, thus skimming along like lightning, the crews cool and determined, followed each other in awful silence."

As he looked back from the foot of the rapids while he and every man crossed themselves and paused to catch their breath, Fraser knew that here was a cataract that should always be portaged—if a portage were possible.

Again the Tauten chief, not pleased that his advice was continually ignored, warned Fraser that he could go no farther by canoe. On a sketch on a spit of river sand, he indicated a dreadful chain of rapids cutting through mountain passes where, even on foot, it was impossible to travel without climbing up and down precipices sometimes so steep that the Indians used rope ladders.

Still Fraser determined to go on, having found a local Indian guide. Each mile, each river bend, opened glimpses of rougher country, with small trees near the river and, in the barren distance, great, lonely Ponderosa pine. The mountains loomed higher, their peaks gleaming cold in the late afternoon sun. The river became continuous white rapids worse than the

Couvert and spiked by jagged rock.

"I scarcely ever saw anything so dreary, and seldom so dangerous in any country," said Fraser, when his local guide insisted they could go no farther. They camped near today's Leon Creek where, after supper, Fraser forced himself to open his journal. "At present while I am writing this, whatever way I turn, mountains upon mountains, whose summits are covered with eternal snows, close the gloomy scene."

Yet despite the forbidding mountains and the fearful river, he estimated they had travelled thirty miles since the *Rapide Couvert*. The water level, judging from the high water mark, had recently dropped a good ten feet: that was encouraging. Hoping against hope that he would not be forced to abandon the canoes, Fraser again deferred making a decision until the morning. The Atnah and Tauten guides wanted to go on on foot to visit the Lillooet. Fraser made no objection. He and his men would remain at the present camp so long as there was a possibility of continuing even a few more miles by canoe.

Apparently the terrifying pain in his groin had eased. It would not be a factor in tomorrow's decision to continue by canoe or to go overland. Simon Fraser wasted no thought on the possibility of abandoning the trip.

Four
Decision

Fraser was continuing his journey without canoes because
the river was impassable and the mountains too rugged
for portaging. How far they would have to
travel by land he did not know.

*T*he old chief repeated his warning: the river was impassable. The Atnah guide and interpreter and the Tauten had "absolutely wanted to leave us and go on on foot to the next nation." Fraser suspected that his own men were of the same mind.

For himself, he did not want to believe any of them.

Simon Fraser had two impelling reasons for wanting to follow this treacherous river to the sea, and probably he could not have separated them had he tried. He was an explorer, eager to see what lay around the next bend on every river he travelled. But his explorations depended on the fortunes of the North West Company with which his own future was inextricably associated. Unfortunately, this first joint-stock company on the North American continent had done so well since its incorporation some twenty-five years earlier that it had already aroused strong competition.

The first major competitor had been the rival Montreal XY Company which had been absorbed three years ago, thereby giving the North West Company control of the entire Canadian fur trade. It had offices in London and New York and Boston, forward depots at Fort William and Lac la Pluie, trading posts strung across the known north-west, and its own fleet of ships on the Great Lakes. Sea-going ships were being outfitted to sail around the Horn for trade with the ports that would be developed when the overland route to the Pacific was finally confirmed. From those ports the North West Company planned to establish trade with China and the Far East.

The second major competitor, the Hudson's Bay Company, had not been as readily absorbed as the XY. The London-based Company chartered by Charles II in 1670 had caused the Nor'Westers little concern until Mackenzie's trip to the Pacific had proved that there was a potential overland route to the gateway to the Far East. Now, the English firm, especially interested in the lucrative beaver and otter trade, was rousing itself for a stake in whatever gain the magnificent discovery might lead to, aided by its strong advantage in owning a monopoly of all lands drained by rivers flowing into Hudson Bay. By way of Hudson Bay, it could send goods to the heart of the continent at half the cost to the Canadians who still had to depend on their ever-lengthening river route from Montreal. In fact, every river the Nor'Westers explored added to their transportation costs.

The English shareholders of the Hudson's Bay Company naturally refused to share their great advantage. The Canadians as naturally met the English competition with all the force of their swiftly developing north-west spirit.

While Fraser was exploring the river he hoped was the Columbia, the North West Company's chief executive, William McGillivray, who had taken his first steps to success in the fur trade as a clerk in the Indian country, was in London trying to persuade Parliament to recognize a fact obvious to all colonials: the Hudson's Bay Company monopoly to exclusive use of Hudson Bay was totally unfair to other British interests. When that appeal failed, he tried to lease rights to sail into the northern bay. At the same time he was offsetting the effects of the

Napoleonic War, which was currently closing one European port after another to trade, by dealing through New York. There he had already bought some trade-goods through the firm headed by John Jacob Astor and sold furs in Asia through Astor's agency.

Paradoxically, Astor was also the Nor'Westers' third big competitor, and the toughest. The stocky German emigrant had already succeeded in several American ventures and had recently announced his intention to make his fortune in the north-west fur trade. As a competitor to the Montrealers he was as challenging, and as unfair, as the Hudson's Bay Company. He was free to outfit his new expedition in Montreal and to engage Canadian canoemen with the support and recognition of the rapidly strengthening American government. With no government backing the Canadians had little to rely on except their own superb determination and enterprise. Truly, McGillivray's great hope of survival was to flout the monopoly and cut transportation costs by the discovery of a navigable river that would link up with the Pacific, and he had no time to waste.

A fourth competitor was the American government itself. The United States, founded only a decade before the North West Company, had recently purchased the territory of Louisiana from France. To determine the size of that territory, believed to be very extensive, and to preempt such industry as it might support, President Thomas Jefferson had outfitted Captain Meriwether Lewis and John Clark. The two had crossed the continent in 1805. As Fraser and every other Nor'Wester knew, all the American high-sounding talk about territorial expansion actually resolved itself into a goal identical with their own, more business.

The English to the north, the Americans to the south, and the Russians to the west—that was the situation haunting Fraser in his tiny tent beside the raging river. He did not know much about the Russians except that they were able seamen, good colonizers, and competent traders who had already established a lucrative business in furs which they were rapidly expanding southward along the coast.

He was a weary and lonely man that night as he struggled to make his paddle-worn hands grasp the quill and his mind control his troubled thoughts. Only two men within hundreds of miles could appreciate the magnitude of the challenge he faced, but Stuart lacked his superior's sense of responsibility and Quesnel was too young and too inexperienced.

It was almost dark in the deep river valley, except for a great shaft of setting sunlight cutting in from the west through the gap made by Leon Creek. Then the stars came out, incredibly bright over Fraser's camp which might have been at the bottom of a well. The cold crept down from the high snows, as chilling as the river itself.

Still hoping to continue by the river, in the morning Fraser sent two men to reconnoitre. They were back by ten o'clock. Their report confirmed the often-repeated warnings.

He was not a man to waste time once the decision was forced on him. Here they must cache the canoes, the surplus trade goods, and such provisions as they absolutely would not need. Under the hot June sun that heated the valley to the temperature of a bake-oven the men again gathered driftwood and constructed stout scaffolds. The *Perseverance* and the three other Company canoes were hoisted onto the scaffolds, each covered by branches against wind and rain and sun. Voyageurs sweated as they dug great pits and in them buried "such other articles as we could not carry along."

The men begged Fraser to cache most of the dried salmon. The Indians had assured them that plenty of fresh and dried salmon could be traded from the Lillooet at the next native village, and the two voyageurs who had reconnoitred during the hours from dawn until ten o'clock had told their fellows how bad the trail was ahead. "[They] thought it a hardship to carry an overplus of provisions & therefore insisted upon leaving part of their charge."

Fraser listened as patiently as he could, knowing he must not risk travelling without an adequate supply of food: "While we have a salmon remaining, bad as they are, there will be nothing impossible for us to do."

After the second night at the Leon Creek camp, everyone was up long before the mist cleared from the river. In the thick fog that hid the mountains crowding in on every side, Fraser put his men to work digging more pits. Although he trusted the local Indians, he was cagey enough not to trust anyone completely, and this time he ensured that the Indians were not present. Because "our acquaintanceship with them was too slight to merit implicit confidence . . . such articles as we should absolutely require upon our return" were secretly buried. For the men who wanted to cache all the salmon, he had a characteristic reply: "To this I could not with propriety consent."

Fraser was continuing his journey, without canoes because

the river was impassable and the mountains too rugged for portaging. How far they would have to travel by land he did not know. Certainly it would be no farther than he could help. When the river again became navigable he would barter for other canoes and continue the journey as planned.

In the meantime, despite his recent indisposition, he would ask no man to do more than he himself. Guns they must have and pistols. Each man carried his own, and the ammunition. "By 5 A.M. all was ready & each took charge of his own package weighing each about 80 lbs. of indispensable necessaries." Among them, they carried almost a ton.

Five

"What Cannot Be Cured, Must Be Endured"

*"Our situation is critical and highly unpleasant;
however we shall endeavour to make the best of it;
what cannot be cured, must be endured."*

On that first morning below Leon Creek, each man easily shouldered his eighty-pound pack. Eighty pounds was nothing for a voyageur accustomed to at least two ninety-pound packs, nor, probably, was it for Fraser. They plodded along looking like apes, arms swinging free, up and down a succession of steep ravines, heads bent low to hold the tump-lines supporting the packs on their shoulders. After a couple of miles the packs began to feel heavy, and heads to ache from the pressure of the leather bands. Gradually it dawned on every man that there would be no canoes waiting at the lower end of the rapids. Instead of dumping the packs, flexing neck and shoulder muscles, and relieving the monotony of carrying with the rhythm of the paddle-stroke, they must continue on foot. The swinging gait changed to a steady slogging and then to sheer, painful drudgery.

All day they trudged along on legs unaccustomed to prolonged walking. For almost the entire duration of the portage the men, accustomed to travelling on water, could not catch even a glimpse of the river they hoped to explore. It was far below the aboriginal path they followed and sometimes as much as a mile away. Even those who had wanted to go overland shared Fraser's longing to get back in canoes.

"Still indulging the fond hopes of discovering an opening for making use of canoes," Fraser and Stuart clambered down to the river while the men prepared the evening camp-fires. They returned without any immediate hope. "The channel was deep, cut through rocks of immense heighth, and forming eddies and gulphs, which it was impossible for canoes even to approach with safety."

Next day, outcroppings of broken rock marred the trail through comparatively level country. Sharp stones cut through stout moccasins. As the sun shone hotter with every hour and the men's pace slackened, one brief, terse phrase lodged in Fraser's mind for later jotting in his journal. In the jargon of the day, "All hands had blistered feet!"

This was a new phase of exploring the unknown river, these miles of dry, short-grass plateaus between the mountains. Only an occasional picturesque Ponderosa pine broke the monotony of the landscape. As the men trudged along that excruciatingly difficult trail, the river might never have existed.

Hour after hour the sun beat down on the straggling men, its heat trapped in the wide valley-like plateau. It tortured the eyes. Lips became parched and tongues swollen. The sight of a small green oasis, rising like a mirage in a desert, suddenly hastened every lagging step; green brush must mean moisture. The first voyageurs at the oasis fell on their knees and clawed a small depression with their hands. While the sluggish water seeped into it, they scooped up the liquid in their dirty palms. As quickly they spat it out. Longing for cool, clear mountain water, they had come instead on a warm sulphur spring, bitter-tasting and nauseating, "some of which, However, we drank."

By sheer moral strength Fraser kept them trudging on until late afternoon when they met a small band of Lillooet. They bartered with the Indians to obtain enough food for supper. The Lillooet also helped carry packs for the more seriously exhausted voyageurs. At sunset the white men camped well beyond the Indians beside a small stream flowing in from the west. There, while Fraser kept watch, the voyageurs dropped to their bellies beside the clear mountain stream, palming up great gulps to replace body moisture sweated out during the day. Too hungry to complain about lingering discomforts, every man grabbed for the good Lillooet food, ". . . different kinds of Roots, wild onions formed into syrope, excellent dried salmon, and some berries."

The Lillooet—Fraser usually referred to them as Askettih—took their name from the Indian word meaning wild onion. They lived along the river below Leon Creek where they did a little beaver-trapping.

Through his interpreters Fraser asked them many questions which they willingly answered. He spent considerable time interrogating one old Lillooet, a "very talkative fellow . . . [who] had been to the sea; saw *great canoes* and white men." The talkative fellow tried to describe the deep-sea ships he had seen and the fine clothes worn by the proud white men who sailed them. Clapping his hands on his hips, he strutted around the riverside camp trying to imitate their manner.

But how far was it from here to the sea? Fraser begged to know. How many nights' journey?

The old Lillooet said it was only ten days' journey to the sea from the main Lillooet village, which was three days distant. Thirteen days. Perhaps two weeks. Fraser rejoiced in the hope of reaching his destination so soon even while he wondered if he and his men could last that long.

On the third day below Leon Creek the trail was so bad he

thought they might never reach the Lillooet village; the Pacific Ocean seemed hopelessly remote. That day the country through which they passed was "the most savage that can be imagined, yet we were always in a beaten path and always in Sight of the river, which, however, we could not approach," so steep and forbidding were its rocky banks. But at least they could see the river again, and the country had changed; there were more trees and more fresh-water streams and the heat, while still intense, was slightly tempered by more abundant vegetation.

The relief was so slight as to make little difference to either Indian or white man. The Indians, who yesterday had helped transport the packs with their two horses, today declined to carry anything. They were, they said, too hot and tired to help. Several were in a noticeably surly mood. When they paused for a brief noon break, one of the guides laid down his loaded gun beside him; a second later an inquisitive Lillooet reached for it, his hand straying unwittingly to the trigger. The guide thrust the weapon upward so that it exploded into the air, the report echoing and re-echoing ominously from mountain to mountain. The loud report failed to alarm several of the younger braves. Later in the day, they donned war-paint and charged that the white men were enemies in disguise. Because they refused to put down their bows and arrows at their chief's order, Fraser staged another of his periodic shows of strength. He and his clerks and guides fired a great, noisy volley into the air. That seemed to have the required effect on the Indians, and it may have helped to calm his own inner fears about his uneasy situation.

Probably to divert the thoughts of his men, as well as his own, he also staged one of his rare place-naming ceremonies at the end of the long, gruelling day.

"Encampt at a considerable river, which flows from the right, and which we called Shaw's River." The name did not survive, but something about today's Bridge River may have reminded Fraser of the partner who had been a *bourgeois* when he spent his first years in the north-west as a lonely, inexperienced clerk. Angus Shaw had recently retired east to a more comfortable department and had married William McGillivray's sister.

Not far below the Bridge River and across a deep, tumultuous rapids, Fraser saw the main Lillooet village, high on the left bank. He saw it and yet at the same time really did not see it. His attention had been caught by the sight of a great, branchless tree, swirling in a whirlpool so powerful and so deep that its surface looked as smooth as oil. The tree was longer than any one of the canoes he had left cached back near Leon Creek, and broader. Steadily, powerless, it swung round and round as he watched. It was still in the same position when he jerked his eyes away from it minutes later. It might stay there for ever, till the force of the water wore it to nothing. So too might a canoe, and its crew.

Yet, to his amazement and delight, only half a mile farther on, the river again became comparatively calm and he saw canoes drawn up on a stretch of beach. They were not the familiar birch-bark canoes, but heavier craft made from a great single length of spruce bark. After feasting his eyes on them from a great enough distance not to antagonize the Lillooet owners, Fraser looked to the village crowning a fine bench. But he did not yet go close. Remembering the young braves' earlier hostility, he chose for his own camp a spot on the opposite bank that could readily be defended. Then, while his men were setting up camp, he went down to the river's edge to talk to the large party of Lillooet who had paddled across, obviously wishing to shake hands, "at least one hundred & thirty seven men." Among them were many older men who, he hoped, might be less eager for a fight than the young braves and who doubtless had heard about the great, noisy volley. Fraser marched unhesitatingly to the Lillooet chief and shook his hand. Then, with the help of the Tauten chief and two other interpreters, he assured the Lillooet that he had come as a friend and that he was going to follow the river to the sea.

The Lillooet were so definite in their assurance that the river was navigable to the sea that Fraser doubted their claim. So did his Tauten and Atnah friends. In the midst of mountains soaring to great snow-covered peaks, the opposite seemed far more likely.

That day Fraser did not stress his determination to go to the sea. Next morning, he wished he had said more about it, or taken another approach. For days, ever since the *Rapide Couvert*, the Tauten and Atnah guides had urged him not to go on by the river. The mere mention of his plan to continue despite their well-meaning advice was more than they could bear. During the night they quietly left. Much as he regretted the fact that he had not paid them for their services, he wondered even more how he could get along without them.

"Here we are, in a strange Country, surrounded with dangers, and difficulties, among numberless tribes . . . who never had seen the face of a white man. Our situation is critical and highly unpleasant; however we shall endeavour to make the best of it; what cannot be cured, must be endured."

Ever at his most resourceful in an emergency, Fraser put on a bold face. Using sign language and as many words as he and the Lillooet had in common, he arranged to be paddled across the river, taking with him a pack of trade goods.

He found a surprisingly substantial, stockaded long house, "100 by 24 feet," where he was ceremoniously welcomed by the Lillooet chief and his leading men, all well dressed in leather garments similar to those worn by the Atnah. The sight of several manufactured articles encouraged him to hope that the ocean might, after all, be as close as he had been led to believe; a new copper tea-kettle and a large gun, apparently of Russian origin, could only have come from the Pacific. In everything the Lillooet were so well provided for that Fraser's laboriously transported articles and his assurance that soon he would return to set up trading-posts along the river evoked only a cool response.

He needed at least four of their spruce-bark canoes to continue the trip by water. The Lillooet either had only as many as they required for their own use or they shrewdly realized how desperate was Fraser's plight. For hours he harangued the head men at the village, never for a second showing the slightest evidence of his growing frustration. At midday, when he should have been long on the water, the chief suddenly agreed to let him have one canoe. Only one. For it he wanted a kettle and an awl. Fraser willingly paid his price. One canoe was better than none. One canoe would carry the heaviest packs, allowing the men on foot to travel faster. Most important, the expedition would again be back on the river, if only with a token crew.

He got the heaviest packs stowed aboard the strange craft in charge of Stuart, accompanied by two local Indians and a voyageur. He was not unduly apprehensive for their safety because the Lillooet obviously paddled this stretch of river frequently. Just as Stuart was ready to push off, the unpredictable Lillooet chief decided the canoe was overloaded; the voyageur must get out. Though he did not consider the canoe overloaded, Fraser dared not risk a protest that might make the chief change his mind and keep the canoe. Well aware of his dependence on the Indians' advice, he resorted to his only effective weapon under the circumstances, a fine show of courage. Standing steady and sturdy in front of his men, he watched and waved as his friend, and the expedition's second-in-command, was paddled into the unknown, swift current. Stuart, too, rose bravely to the occasion as he acknowledged his superior's good wishes. Aware of Fraser's unspoken concern, he called out a cheery: "Think nothing of it!"; he would meet Fraser at the lower end of the first rapid.

Quickly the rest of the party shouldered their packs and guns and, accompanied by several Lillooet, hurried on as fast as the rough terrain permitted. This was a situation Fraser dreaded, having his men separated. With every toilsome mile his apprehension grew, even before he reached the first rapids; the pack that two days ago had not seemed too heavy for his strong shoulders now became an unbearable burden.

Stuart was not at the first rapids. Nor at the second. Faced with the dreadful prospect of further dividing his party and with growing fears for his friend's safety, Fraser turned his pack over to the men. Taking only his gun and pistol, he trudged on over the trail that was so rough it forced his mind off his worst fears.

Not until he had gone ten heart-breaking miles did he see the canoe at an Indian camp. Stuart was safe. Unable to converse with his Indian paddlers, he could not let them know about stopping. Like Fraser, he realized to what extent his safety had depended on their respect for the white man's courage. Without further words, the two solemnly gripped hands.

Stuart's safe passage in that single Lillooet canoe proved that the river was again navigable. Next day Fraser had the good fortune to trade for another canoe, old and in need of repair, but usable. For it he gave a sick Indian a dose of medicine. A knife purchased the services of a guide, and again Fraser watched from the shore. His second Lillooet canoe held only five men, but he hoped he was steadily improving his situation. Still apprehensive about having his party separated, he accompanied the rest of them along the high, narrow, rocky path where every step seemed more perilous than the one before it.

They were not the only people travelling that ancient trail. Seldom were they out of sight of the smoke of Indian camp-fires close to the river. On the path Fraser had several opportunities to talk to new Indians, and one meeting led to an introduction to a party of Hacamaugh, the natives who lived below the Lillooet.

With the Hacamaugh was a wandering Chilcotin, whose language was familiar to the white men. The Chilcotin said he had been to the sea, and drew a chart showing Fraser the river's course. Again, it was a very rough chart, indicating stretches that seemed impassable. Fraser took it as no good omen that the Chilcotin, the second native who claimed to have been to the

Pacific, after agreeing to accompany the expedition as guide, changed his mind overnight. He was encouraged by the fellow's statement that the ocean was only ten nights distant.

The Hacamaugh, like the Lillooet, had canoes, a fact which suggested that navigation must still be possible for some distance. Their canoes, hollowed or carved from trees, were stranger to the *Canadien* voyageurs than any they had ever seen. Fraser badly needed at least two more canoes to get his entire party back onto the river, but he found the Hacamaugh as unwilling to barter as the Lillooet had been. They listened to his eloquent persuasion, looked over his trade goods, and agreed only to give him passage to the next village, the main Hacamaugh establishment three miles downstream. Their price for the trip was an awl. Fraser decided it would not be expedient to reject the offer, and handed over the awl. Anxiously he took his place with those of his men under Quesnel in the two Lillooet canoes on the river; the others trudged along the trail with Stuart. In quick time, so strong were the rapids, he was landed at a tributary coming in on the east, which the Indians called Camchin. It was the largest tributary he had yet seen.

They all camped down near the shore, in sight of the much larger Hacamaugh village on a high bench across the river. Next morning, accompanied by several of his men in their best shirts and *ceintures fléchées*, Fraser had himself paddled across to visit yet another powerful chief.

The Hacamaugh chief waited for him at the water-side and, after a formal welcome, escorted him up the steep bank to the village, "where his people were sitting in rows, to the number of twelve hundred; and I had to shake hands with all of them."

After the seemingly endless hand-shaking had been completed, the chief "made a long harangue, in course of which he pointed to the sun, to the four quarters of the world and then to us." This was the sort of ceremony Fraser enjoyed when he had time for it or when the ceremony promised to provide food or protection or canoes. Now, needing all three, he listened with close attention to the speeches, which were eloquent, and admired the delivery, which he thought "extremely handsome." He shook hands with the chief's aged father, a querulous blind man who repeatedly stretched out his groping hands to feel those of the white stranger.

After several hours of ceremonial speeches, Fraser and his clerks enjoyed a feast of "salmon, berries, oil and roots in abundance, and our men had six dogs." The wild dogs were a favourite dish of the voyageurs, who had gone hungry often enough to relish a good meal. That night the Indians danced and sang to entertain the visitors.

During the day, Fraser had used every opportunity to press his offer to purchase canoes. He thought about it in his tiny tent at night, and in the morning renewed his offers.

The Hacamaugh listened politely. They accepted every gift. But they avoided committing themselves to a price, or to parting with the coveted means of transportation. The only thing Fraser could be sure of was that "the road ahead was very bad." Despite the Hacamaugh entertainment, he dared not let himself feel any great hope, either of getting canoes or of getting to the sea.

No matter how kind and co-operative the Indians might seem, he felt he could never trust any of them entirely. Yet he had to depend on them—that fact he could never forget, especially with his goal so close. In the midst of these powerful, well-supplied Hacamaugh, much depended on diplomacy, on matching the implied threat of his own resources of arms against their control of the river. "It is certain," Fraser confided to his journal, "the less familiar we are with one another the better for us."

Six
"Thomson's River"

"From an idea that our friends [David Thompson and others]
of the Fort des Prairies *department are established upon
the sources of it, among the mountains, we gave it
the name of Thomson's River.*" The slip in spelling the
Welshman's name was understandable.

*F*raser spent only one night and part of two days near the site of the future town of Lytton, at the confluence of two great, unnamed rivers. He needed a week or more to question the Hacamaugh and to record their answers. His hands were too horny from gripping a paddle and chipping steps out of rock to hold a quill easily. He had to force himself to concentrate on putting words on paper, always conscious that paper was scarce. But one unexpected sight at the Indian village evoked such exciting possibilities that he had to make a note of it.

More observant than the average fur trader, Fraser the explorer missed little of significance wherever he stopped. Having seen a couple of manufactured items at the Lillooet village, he was intrigued to see others here. Expecting them also to have come inland from the Pacific, he examined each carefully. They were European manufactured goods, but certainly they had never been near the Pacific.

He looked at the copper tea-kettle handed him by its proud Hacamaugh owner, turned it over in his hand, studied the manufacturer's stamp. A brass camp-kettle in turn received the same wondering appraisal. So did a torn strip from an ordinary blanket of the sort used by the voyageurs, and sometimes traded for furs.

Where had these articles come from? How had the Hacamaugh obtained them? he asked, suppressing his growing incredulity.

The Hacamaugh said the kettles and the strip of blanket had not come from the Pacific; they had been acquired in trade far up the Camchin. The information partially confirmed the idea slowly forming in Simon Fraser's thoughts, but he dismissed it as being entirely improbable. Minutes later, he knew he must be right.

It was not a European-manufactured trade item that wholly confirmed his growing delight in a wonderful discovery; it was simply items of "cloathing such as the Cree women wear."

With a Métis wife whom he had married *au façon du nord* only the previous year, and children by another Métis girl, he knew the difference between garments worn by women east of the Rockies and those typical of the Pacific slope. He knew that the garments he saw on Hacamaugh women had been made by Indian women far away—how far he could only guess. Those head-bands, beaded tunics, belts, and moccasins could only have come from a North West Company post "beyond the Mountains." They must have come from one of the posts established by David Thompson, somewhere beyond the sources of the Saskatchewan River, and were perhaps the work of Thompson's Métis wife, Charlotte, who usually travelled with him.

Ever eager to tell a white man things he obviously wished to know, the Hacamaugh described at great length their journeys far up the Camchin. They told him about the dry plateau through which it flowed, about the horses that were almost as useful as canoes, and about the bands of strange Indians with whom they traded for furs, skins, and ornaments—and European copper and brass kettles, Fraser reminded them, and clothes such as the Cree women wear.

He felt almost certain that the manufactured goods had come from one of Thompson's posts; from their trademarks, they had been made by an English firm from whom the Nor'Westers regularly imported kettles. What he could not learn was how far away those posts were. Nor could the Hacamaugh tell him whether or not the Camchin, rushing near by through its deep rocky gorge into the river he was exploring, was Thompson's river.

For Fraser those few treasured articles and their probable significance made the Hacamaugh village one of the most important places on the entire trip so far. They suggested the possibility of practical commerce with areas in the interior to the east. If goods reached the Hacamaugh from the interior, men must be able to reach the interior from Hacamaugh territory.

Nowhere since leaving Fort George had he seen a better site for a trading-post. The Hacamaugh, like the Lillooet, were not likely to become important trappers, but they could provide provisions if communications were established between the ocean and the interior. They appeared to have a bountiful supply of food. He had eaten some of the roots dug by the women which they said could be used fresh and baked, or dried and later boiled. They had fresh-caught and dried salmon (salmon roe wrapped in grass and stored in pits until it was nearly rotten, when it "tasted like European cheese," was a great delicacy), venison, and wild dogs, and an abundance of wild berries, nuts, and herbs for flavouring. Their clothes were well made of leather and woven sage-brush or willow bark; they wore cloaks of woven sage and cedar bark to keep off the rain; their moccasins with the tough black-tailed deerskin soles were extremely well made, with cross-strips sewn to the soles to prevent slipping on mountain trails. Fraser needed many pairs of such obviously practical footwear.

The Hacamaugh were also good travellers. They had horses. They were accustomed to using a form of tump-line to carry bundles up and down mountain trails, a wide band made of cedar bark lined with goat's wool.

The more Simon Fraser saw of the Hacamaugh, the more they suggested a possible link with Thompson. It was a sober, frustrating thought, for he probably had not seen his fellow explorer since they had left Fort William three years earlier, so rare and difficult were communications between Fort Chipewyan on the Upper Peace and Thompson's headquarters at Rocky Mountain House far up the Saskatchewan.

Seldom had he chafed more hopelessly against the lack of communication that was a major hardship of the early nineteenth century in the north-west. A letter sent from one post to the other by a courier on snowshoes might be acknowledged when the canoes brought up the supplies and reports from Fort William six months or more later. Generally, all communications from the various river highways were funnelled down to the base on Lake Superior to be sorted, read, commented on, and forwarded. If the letter missed connections, it might reach its intended destination eighteen months or even two years later. Men became almost as hungry for news as for food. They hoarded every scrap of information, mulling it over and filling in the frustrating blanks with their imaginations. In much the same way they had to rely on their imaginations for the details of weather and terrain in newly explored territory: there were no maps.

Fraser was more fortunate than most of his partners. He at least knew that Thompson was exploring a river somewhere to the east. Was it, perhaps, more easily navigable than this river on which he, Fraser, was about to continue his perilous way? Was it more like the rivers east of the Rockies where a man could enjoy wondering about what lay around the next bend instead of concentrating on survival?

Much would depend on his and Thompson's information, when it was eventually pieced together at Fort William, in Montreal, or on the drawing-tables of European cartographers. The information might confirm the goal glimpsed by mariners when Jacques Cartier sailed into the St. Lawrence, or perhaps even before Columbus first sailed west. The French had named the little bay where they launched their canoes above Montreal *La Chine*. From *La Chine* they hoped to reach China. And when the French relinquished the quest it had been taken up chiefly by men with whom they enjoyed great rapport, the Highland Scots.

Those Highland Scots in the North West Company, with a few Americans, Englishmen, and the Welsh David Thompson, had followed the canoe routes opened by Radisson and La Vérendrye. Using the French language and key Indian terms— the words for canoe, snowshoe, tump-line, and pemmican were the most important—they had moved from band to band, usually in safety except when they were caught in tribal wars, or became too reckless under the influence of rum, or invited trouble by enticing another man's woman. The Nor'Westers had already explored much of the north-west, at their own expense, and most of it during Fraser's time.

Now he was on his way to the Pacific, as was Thompson, and neither could know for a year or more which one got there first, if either ever succeeded. Fraser's immediate concern was to trade for a couple of the Hacamaugh dug-out canoes with the carved bows gaily painted black, white, or red that beckoned from a snug beach above his river. He had little time to wonder whether the Hacamaugh's sturdy canoes meant that the river below was worse than stretches he had already survived.

On the morning of June 20 the Hacamaugh chief agreed to let Fraser have two canoes and, in a typical burst of Indian generosity, offered personally to conduct the explorer part of the way. He also offered the services of several young men to help carry the packs, and a diminutive guide who soon became known as the Little Fellow. For canoes and men and guidance Fraser was profoundly grateful; during the five days since leaving the Lillooet village he had covered only forty miles.

As usual, many Indians gathered at the riverside to see the little party embark. While his voyageurs were inspecting the strange dug-outs and learning how to stow the cargo aboard them, he displayed a couple of packs of assorted trade-goods, the first tiny trade fair on the Pacific slope.

There could be little hope of doing any worth-while bartering, and he had the two canoes. Something else was in his mind, a vague hope that later found expression in his journal:

"I showed the Indians some trading articles and asked for leather, but none was brought. I gave the chief a large knife and an awl, and he expressed his favour in thanks and affability. I also gave a few trinkets to an Indian of a different nation in order that he might show them to his friends."

Who was the Indian of a different tribe? Did Fraser hope he might have some contact with the upper Camchin, the river that might lead to Thompson's territory? Watching the great tributary from the east disappear into the roaring river he had been following for weeks, an overwhelming longing to communicate with his fellow explorer forced Fraser to pause briefly.

Thompson might never know they had been so close to one another, if in fact they were close. Neither might survive to inform the other. But a man did not become an explorer without faith in himself and in the eventual success of his mission. No matter how devoutly he put his trust in God, he also propitiated fate, especially if he were a *bourgeois* long familiar with the superstitious customs of the voyageur.

The natives called the river from the east Camchin. For good luck, perhaps, Fraser chose something more sentimental. "From an idea that our friends of the *Fort des Prairies* department are established upon the sources of it, among the mountains, we gave it the name of Thomson's River." The slip in spelling the Welshman's name was understandable.

Seven
"Where No Human Being Should Venture"

The voyageur had regained consciousness on a short,
easy current with only half of the canoe in his arms.
He had been hurled onto a rock, sucked back into the river
by a great wave, and then thrown clear by a second wave.

"*A*bout 10 A.M. we embarked. Now all our people were in canoes."

This was the moment Fraser had been hoping for ever since he cached his birch-bark canoes. Like a solemn vow renewed, the occasion recalled the high resolve of the first morning at Fort George. As his two Lillooet canoes swept into the current with the two dug-outs and a following of Indians, he might have been William McGillivray himself, master of a fine entourage. But the river had long since ceased to be the comparatively peaceful course he had embarked on three weeks ago. Every roaring mountain stream had increased its volume. Every mile of rock through which it had battered its way had added to its fury. The newly named Thompson River, roaring out of the great flume it had cut through its own unknown miles of rock, doubled the raging water mass and the travellers' peril. Racing along with the current at a speed faster than any he had ever known, he had no time to rejoice in his good fortune—if it was good fortune—or in the presence of the Hacamaugh chief and the three Hacamaugh guides. He had no time to hope he was on the last leg of his trip to the sea.

"Aided by heavy rapids and a strong current, we in a short time, came to a portage." That was the way with this river; it lured men on with a swift, exciting run that invariably ended in a toilsome portage, each more hazardous than the one before.

For long minutes before the Hacamaugh chief indicated a

landing-place, Fraser had been watching, every muscle tensed, for some means of escaping the fury of the foaming, jaundiced demon clutching at his canoe. Without a second or a yard to spare, the first three canoes were successfully beached. The fourth, caught in a great, swirling eddy, was swamped. In the swift action of the minutes that followed, no one could have said exactly what happened. Men scrambled and were helped out of the water. The canoe was raised, emptied, and hauled clear. Most of the packs were also saved, though a count later revealed that several had been carried away.

Then Fraser looked for the portage trail.

For the first hundred yards or so it was reasonably discernible as it climbed a long, steep grade. Toward the crest it petered out in a vast slide of loose rock and stones, sloping sharply down to the water's edge. On this slide, the Hacamaugh told Fraser, several of their people had perished when they lost their balance, a fact ominously confirmed by the many grave-mounds in the area, each surmounted by piles of the small, rolling stones that obliterated each season's trail. These unfortunate men and women had been Indians and unknown to the white men. But the sudden sight of one of his own men slithering down the slope brought the significance of those grave-mounds close to Fraser; fortunately the voyageur saved himself by catching hold of a firm, jagged rock. His fellows muttered a fervent "Hail Mary" as a kettle on top of the man's pack broke loose and, bouncing clamorously off rock after rock, plummeted into the river which instantly sucked it out of sight.

That day, the familiar four points of the compass gave way to new directions. Instead of looking to the accustomed north, south, east, and west, the eyes of every man looked up to the snow-peaked mountain tops, down to the Siren river, forward over those treacherous rocks, back to toils too well remembered.

They did not go back. Over this trail, despite its hazards, Indians had travelled for a thousand years or more. Over it, next morning, the men carried two of the canoes and part of the cargo before stopping for breakfast. After breakfast, while Quesnel guarded the forward packs and the voyageurs carried the remaining canoes and cargo, Fraser and Stuart paused to write up the journal and log. They had not completed the book-work when they were "alarmed by the loud bawling of our guides": the men were lost in the rapids!

But they had already carried the canoes part way along the trail and were supposed to be bringing up the remaining cargo. Locking their writing cases, Fraser and Stuart hurried to investigate.

They found Quesnel downstream, guarding the packs. None of the men were with him and, where four canoes ought to have been, three were missing. Fraser soon spotted one across the river, on shore with some of the men. The other canoes and the other voyageurs could only be somewhere ahead, on the river or lost in it.

Fraser and Stuart rushed frantically along the trail for almost four miles before they passed a voyageur, who thought his fellows were following. A little farther on they saw another, D'Alaire, coming slowly toward them, leaning heavily on a stick and soaking wet. At first he could whisper only a few halting words. When he could speak coherently, he confirmed Fraser's growing suspicion: "he and the others finding the carrying place too long and the canoes too heavy, took it upon themselves to venture down by water . . ."

D'Alaire had been in the last canoe to set out, and it had capsized at the first cascade. The bowman and steersman had scrambled free, clinging to the overturned canoe, but he, the middleman, had been caught underneath. "Still having my recollection," he had broken clear as the canoe bounced up when the other two jumped into a stretch of comparatively quiet water to swim ashore. He had then contrived to climb astride the bobbing craft. Balancing it with his body, he had ridden it down a succession of rapids, catching a glimpse of his fellows on the shore. But for the man's exhausted condition, Fraser and Stuart could not have believed his story. "In the second or third cascade (for I cannot remember which) the canoe from a great height plunged into the deep eddy at the foot, and striking with violence against the bottom splitted in two. Here I lost my recollection." The voyageur had regained consciousness on a short, easy current with only half of the canoe in his arms. He had been hurled onto a rock, sucked back into the river by a great wave, and then thrown clear by a second wave.

Surveying the precipice the man had climbed, Fraser marvelled that he had been able to claw his way up. But he could have got out of the river valley in no other way. By Fraser's estimate, he had survived three miles of "rapids, cascades, whirlpools, &c. all inconceivably dangerous." His survival was a miracle.

Not until nightfall did Fraser get his men together, with the help of the Indians, at a canyon campside at the foot of today's Jackass Mountain.

In the morning, one of the voyageurs was ill. Cold rain chilled the spirits of men usually able to ignore the effects of bad weather. The food Fraser was able to obtain in this inaccessible stretch of the canyon, though abundant, was "commonly wretched if not disgusting." Stuart's report that he had seen a snake "as thick as his wrist" increased the apprehensions of men already on the watch for rattlers.

None of these factors threatened the success of the expedition as seriously as the voyageurs' flagrant disobedience. Running canoes they were supposed to carry merited sharp discipline: men had lost a year's pay for less, or had been flogged. But these were reliable, experienced canoemen, who had each paddled four or five thousand miles since leaving Montreal. They knew white water. They were accustomed to carrying canoes, though never dug-outs heavier than a *canot de maître*. "We perceived that one way or another our men were getting out of order. They prefered walking to going by water in wooden canoes, particularly after their late sufferings in the rapids."

Fraser, accustomed to the brutal enforcement of discipline common during the early nineteenth century, refrained from punishment that day. At the end of the portage, where the river was still perilously swift, although safer, according to the Indians, than the precipitous shore, he ordered the canoes to be made ready. Like the others, he remembered those piles of gravestones, and he had seen others along the way. He knew, as perhaps the voyageurs did not, that their survival as well as his own depended even more on their morale than on their skill with a paddle; that their worst enemy lay deep within themselves. It was fear. And fear could be overcome only by an example of courage, his own.

"Therefore I embarked in the bow of a canoe myself and went down several rapids." The gesture heartened every man, white and Indian. During a day that might have broken their morale—one of the voyageurs fell and shattered the canoe he was carrying, and Stuart's canoe filled and was almost lost—the Hacamaugh chief assured Fraser that he would stay with him until he was past the most dangerous places and the Little Fellow agreed to stay all the way to the ocean and back.

Fortunately, he was too busy to think about much but survival. Replacing the canoes lost by the insubordinate voyageurs took time; he had to find canoes and then he had to acquire them. Exultantly, on Friday, June 24, he recorded a significant deal: "This morning traded two canoes for two calico bed gowns." Again his tiny brigade was complete. Before the day ended he had less happy news: "Ran down the canoes; but about the middle of the rapids two of them struck against one another, by which accident one of them lost a piece of its stern, and the steersman his paddle."

Repairing canoes took precious time. So too did the ceremonies performed by successive bands of Indians who sang and danced for the white men, usually early in the morning when Fraser longed to be on his way. Dependent on them as he was for food and transport, he had no choice but to make a show of appreciation. It was a reasonable price for a full belly for himself and his men, including the several Hacamaugh whose help had become indispensable.

For a time, the Hacamaugh had seemed a burden—the chief

and his braves and the Little Fellow, who was now the real guide for the expedition. But, expert as the voyageurs were in canoes, they were poor mountain men. Their comparatively short legs, an asset for a voyageur, were no match for the Indians' strong, long legs and sure feet. Some days, on the worst mountain trails, his voyageurs were actually a liability, their maintenance cutting heavily into Fraser's currency, the trade goods they could no longer carry without help from the Indians.

Below Hell's Gate, the Black Canyon yawned so deep the sun touched the river only when it was directly overhead. Yet here the Hacamaugh chief announced his intention of returning to his village at the inflow of the Thompson. Hoping that the worst at last was almost over, Fraser made him a farewell present of a large silver brooch which he immediately fastened to his head-band. But Fraser was grateful to have the Little Fellow and several Hacamaugh continue with him. Whatever the chief might think, to the white explorer the trail continued to become more hazardous with every mile.

"We were obliged to carry up among loose Stones on the face of a steep hill, over a narrow ridge between two precipices. Near the top where the ascent was perfectly perpendicular, one of the Indians climbed to the summit, and with a long pole drew us up, one after another. This took three hours."

In places, the path was so narrow a man could scarcely find a footing, even moving sideways. Voyageurs fought dizziness and fear so desperately that only later did they discover they had clung so close to the rock wall that their noses and cheeks were painfully bruised and bleeding. On such fearful stretches Fraser was wholly dependent on the Indians. "We were obliged to hand our guns from one to another, and where the greatest precaution was required to pass even singly, the Indians went through boldly with loads."

That night, because there was no convenient village where he could barter for food, the Indians tried to net salmon. They took five, "which divided among forty persons was little indeed, but better than nothing" after so arduous a day in fresh mountain air.

And still the river continued ever more hazardous and the trail worse than anything Fraser had experienced.

"We had to pass where no human being should venture." He meant no fur trader; except on the rock slides, he could easily discern the trail worn by countless generations of Indians. Where the trail broke off at the foot or at the top of a precipice or chasm, the Indians had constructed ladders of poles and boughs, the rungs lashed to the poles with stout bark-rope. The ladders hung "like the shrouds of a ship," one above the other to dizzy heights, secured to rocks and trees by bark-rope. They were safe for the natives, remarked Fraser, "but we, who had not the advantage of their experience, were often in imminent danger, when obliged to follow their example."

Below Spuzzum (Fraser spelt it Spazum, probably following local pronunciation) he met the first of yet another Indian tribe, the Salish or coastal people. The presence of Indians known as coastal people suggested contact with the ocean, but he no longer counted the days until he hoped to reach his goal. So stubborn was his determination to continue to follow the river that he neglected to comment on the possible significance of the Salish. Instead, he wrote a melancholy note in his journal about their tombs on the west bank, "superior to any thing of the kind I ever saw among the savages. They are about fifteen feet long and of the form of a chest of drawers . . . Around the tombs were deposited all the property of the deceased."

His melancholy moment relieved by the acquisition of a couple of damaged canoes and a hearty meal of fresh salmon, berries, oil, and onions provided by the Salish, he would have embarked as soon as the canoes were repaired if the guides had not advised against it. "Sensible, from experience, that a hint from these people is equal to a command, and that they would not follow if we Declined, we remained." But he had the cargo aboard the mended canoes by five o'clock in the morning, when he and every man not engaged in paddling trudged off on foot.

None of them could have carried their packs much farther, even with the help of the Indians. Though the eighty pounds each had shouldered on leaving Leon Creek no longer contained dried salmon and several packs had been lost, what remained had become unbearably heavy, as had their guns.

The respite from carrying was brief. Eight miles farther on the straggling party again reached impassable white water, where the canoes were already being beached. Canoemen, too weary to help with the unloading, dropped to the ground to rest. Fraser, himself nearly exhausted, sent the Little Fellow on in search of food. To his great relief the Hacamaugh returned with a band of unknown Indians carrying quantities of fresh salmon, cooked better than any he had eaten anywhere along the river.

Rested a little and with full bellies, voyageurs and Indians were more readily persuaded to shoulder packs which now felt only half as heavy as when they had been unloaded from the beached canoes abandoned above the rapids. The peaks were still snow-covered, the swirling river too swift and hazardous for canoe travel, but Fraser, more alert than at Spuzzum, had directed their attention to a truly hopeful sign, a great net, some "8 fathoms long" and with meshes sixteen inches wide. Such a net, he said, could only be used to trap large animals, deer and perhaps moose, who frequented woods and open spaces such as they had not seen for weeks. This must surely be an indication that soon the river would break out of the mountains.

The indication became even more likely when, about eleven o'clock, the straggling, foot-sore men crossed a creek where "the main river tumbles from rock to rock between precipices with great violence." Below the precipices the Indians served them more well-cooked salmon—in wooden dishes; none of the mountain tribes had had such dishes. A few miles farther on a "bad rock" marked the place "where the rapids terminate."

At today's Lady Franklin Rock, Fraser was almost out of the mountains. Eight days and approximately sixty gruelling miles below the Thompson, he had reached the first of several well-developed Achinroe or coastal Salish villages.

From here, said the Indians at the village below the rock, the river was navigable to the sea. And, according to the sun and Stuart's findings, they were still travelling almost due south, as they had been ever since leaving Fort George. That was the direction in which Fraser expected the Columbia to flow.

Eight

"The Threat of Our Displeasure"

*A brief, terse entry recorded the greatest achievement
of his lifetime: "At last we came in sight of
a gulph or bay of the sea . . . ."*

*S*o far he had had no need, and little opportunity, to consult his carefully copied notes about the Pacific Coast. Below Lady Franklin Rock, near the site of the modern town of Yale, the mountains still soared high, their peaks were still snow-covered. While he had reason to believe that he would soon be out of them, he had considerably less reason to believe that, as the old Lillooet and the wandering Chilcotin had suggested, he would reach the ocean ten days after leaving the Thompson. Already eight of those ten days had passed.

According to his notes, the Columbia flowed into the Pacific at latitude 46°20′. Even if the river continued to flow due south in a great open plain without further bad rapids to delay their progress, it would take more than two days to travel that far. Simon Fraser had no real information about what lay between his present camp-site and that long-sought goal. He could call on no known facts to bolster his own hopes and boost the morale of his men. Everything he had to know he had to learn from questioning these unfamiliar Salish people and from his own exploring.

He had faced the unknown too often and for too long to be discouraged by lack of precise information. To him the unknown was the great challenge, especially when, as at the village below the bad rock, he saw what he wanted more than anything in the world—fine, sturdy canoes, some of them apparently new.

Fraser did not rush to the landing beside a swift creek to

study those canoes; such obvious eagerness would not only increase the price the natives would charge, it would also suggest that he knew little about Indian ways. But long before he could prudently take a good, close look, he had managed several satisfying glances. The canoes were not made of birch or spruce bark. They were dug-outs, larger than those fashioned by the Hacamaugh, and looked as though they had been hollowed with fire. Since the hour was now well past four o'clock, he might have to wait until morning to make an offer for two or more of the canoes. Meantime, the usual Indian ceremonies would provide an opportunity to ask questions as well as to woo their co-operation.

As did every man in his party, Fraser welcomed the initial ceremony that required visitors to eat a good meal. Squatting on the ground in the chief's house, he observed evidences of a culture comparable to that of the more advanced eastern tribes. Such refinements as the salmon cooked in wooden pots by means of heated stones and served in a wooden dish on a neatly woven mat encouraged him to hope that his river must eventually flow through country more agreeable than any he had travelled so far.

While he ate in polite silence, he looked at everything about him, carefully pretending not to do so. He thought the mats and rugs woven from wild goat's wool and dog's hair "equally as good as those found in Canada." *Wattap* hats, with broad, conical brims, worn by men and women, and broad cedar-bark head-bands suggested a potential market for gaily coloured ribbons. Every Indian wore ornaments—shell and brass necklaces and horn bracelets, an indication that they would surely enjoy

European beads. He also observed that the men were well armed with "bows and arrows, spears and clubs or horn Powmagans." There were "few or no christian goods among them, but from their workmanship in wood they must be possessed of good tools at least for that purpose."

Later, when he was invited to inspect the village, he was amazed at the skilful construction of "an excellent house 46 by 23 feet, and constructed like American frame houses" from heavy planks supported on strong, rudely carved posts. Across the river another village with similar houses indicated a general competence. So did the tombs, of which the chief was very proud, particularly a new one built on carved posts. "The sculpture is rudely finished," the explorer observed, "and the posts are covered all over with bright shells, which shine like mercury, but the contents of the tomb emitted a disagreeable stench."

Before Fraser could diplomatically commence his barter for canoes, four Indians paddled downstream to spread the news of the expedition's arrival to their neighbours. Watching their craft disappear around a bend, he shrewdly approved its lines and seaworthiness. In that direction, through that barely discernible gap in the mountains, tomorrow, please God, he too would travel.

During the evening, the Indians danced and sang by flaming torch light, providing Fraser with intimate glimpses of their customs for later inclusion in his journal: "Both sexes are stoutly made, and some of the men are handsome: but I cannot say so much for the women, who seem to be slaves, for in the course of their dances, I remarked that the men were pillaging them from one another."

In the morning Fraser's increasing apprehension was confirmed: like the Lillooet and the Hacamaugh, these people wanted to keep their canoes far more than they wanted anything he had to offer. All he got for his appeals was a passage for himself and his men and the baggage, at the late hour of nine, "some of us with the Indians and others without, just as best suited the Indians."

That day he watched the valley change slowly, widening almost imperceptibly as the canoes swept along with a strong current, between banks "adorned with fine trees." He had no desire to stop when the Indians landed at a small friendly village for a meal and an hour of dancing. "Lost a couple of hours," he complained, chafing under the irksome fact that he was temporarily deprived of his command. To his great relief, in the afternoon they again made good time, but only until five o'clock. At five, the Indians "who favoured us with the canoes thus far, left us and went home, and in consequence we were obliged to encamp."

Their neighbours at the next village were even more hospitable than either of the bands below Lady Franklin Rock. In fact they were so civil that Fraser, eating their sturgeon, oil, and roots, doubted their sincerity, even while he admired their evidences of culture—fine rugs made of dog's hair, dyed and woven very much like Highland plaids; stout, long-handled fishing-nets; and very competent-looking horn spears with great wooden handles. Most of all he was attracted to several articles that must surely have come to them by way of the Pacific Ocean—"a large copper kettle shaped like a jar, and a large English hatchet stamped *Saraget with the figure of a crown*." Had those articles been brought around the Horn by Captain Cook? Or Captain

Vancouver? Or, perhaps, by the American Captain Gray when he sailed into the mouth of the Columbia? The Indians did not know.

That night Fraser and his clerks took turns at standing guard while the men slept on the bank beside the packs, under a sky more open than any they had seen since entering the mountains. In the morning the Indians who owned the European-manufactured goods also declined to sell him a canoe, although, after prolonged persuasion, they too agreed to paddle the party as passengers. Owing either to a misunderstanding or to some caprice of the canoe owners, they landed at eleven o'clock and announced they would go no farther.

Again explorer and interpreters repeated the monotonous, time-consuming appeal for transport and, during the long bartering ceremonies, he met an Indian who said he had been to the ocean. Fraser's suddenly aroused interest waned when the Indian insisted that the ocean was so near that the white men would see it tomorrow. His doubts were confirmed by Stuart's latitude reading, the first since breaking clear of the mountains.

Now Stuart could determine their position without having to use his mercury reflector. The river had flooded into a vast lake that provided a fine natural horizon. The sun was high, the sky clear. On June 30, he found the angle to be 127°23′, which indicated that they were still far north of the fabled outflow of the Columbia. They still had a long way to go.

Three hours after being so unceremoniously landed Fraser's persistent application to the local Salish band obtained a further passage. On a swift, nine-mile run, speeded by a strong current, he watched in continued amazement as the river flooded close to the broad valley's mountainous shoulders. So broad was the flooded river he did not notice three others flowing in on the right, today's Harrison, Stave, and Pitt rivers. He could not believe his eyes when he saw seals; seals, surely, did not come inland? He had no time to think of a name for a large river flowing in on the left, opposite a "round Mountain . . . which the natives called *shemotch*," probably the modern Sumas Peak.

When he camped for the second night since leaving Lady Franklin Rock, under a great cedar on the right bank of the flooded river, Fraser measured its circumference, five fathoms. A tree, "*five fathoms* in circumference" might be expected to grow near the ocean, but there was Stuart's latitude reading; Stuart was not likely to make an error. Even more mystifying was the fact that the river, since breaking free of the mountains, had suddenly changed its course; now it flowed westward. That night he slept little, partly because of his confused thoughts about the recorded information and the evidence at hand, partly because "musketoes are in clouds, & we had little or nothing to eat." Their hunger was due to the local Indians' refusal to provide more food than the white men could carry in their bellies. Even if he or his men had been adept fishermen, they lacked the spears and nets necessary for catching fish in this heavily silted river that teemed with salmon.

On the morning of July 1, the fog lifted by four o'clock, when the party embarked, again as passengers and again only for a few hours. At eight their boatmen landed them at a large village.

Desperately frustrated by the uncertainty of their mode of travel and by the increasing evidence that they were much nearer sea level than he had expected, Fraser appealed to the Little Fellow. The Hacamaugh guide by this time had "assumed an air of consequence from his being of our party; he now ranks with Mr. Stuart, Mr. Quesnel and myself." Perhaps he could make a special plea for less-interrupted travel?

The Little Fellow accompanied the explorer on the ceremonial call on the chief of the latest coastal band. After the chief had presented Fraser with a roll of stout moccasin leather and Fraser had repaid the gift with a "calico gown, for which he was thankful and proud," the Little Fellow made a stirring harangue about the white men and their prowess on the water and on land, their courage and the great guns with which they could defend themselves. The Salish were only mildly interested. They showed so little curiosity at seeing white men and so little fear of their arms that Fraser concluded they must often have seen or heard of men with pale skins. All the Little Fellow's eloquence achieved was a welcome meal of fish, berries, and dried oysters for every man in the expedition.

These Indians were so well off their affluence depressed Fraser even while he marvelled at the results of their skills, evident everywhere in the spacious village. Their cedar-plank houses, built in a block over six hundred feet long and sixty broad, were not only larger, but of finer construction than any he had so far seen. The chief's main apartment was a great room ninety feet long, its ceiling supported by pillars ornamented with carved figures of humans, birds, and animals, with an opening through which smoke from the cooking-fires escaped. On the shore beside the river, he had seen even greater evidence of skilled craftsmanship—several sturdy, seaworthy canoes, each large enough to accommodate his entire party and their baggage.

The Salish reaction to his appeal was what he had come to expect. But Fraser could no longer continue to accept refusal. During the long evening, he and the Hacamaugh renewed their appeal with two significant interruptions. The first came when the clerks called them to see the tide. The tide, "about 2$^{1}/_{2}$ feet," was the first any of them had experienced, and a great source of wonder to the voyageurs from Montreal. The second interruption occurred when Stuart set up his instruments to shoot the stars, the conditions being right for a night latitude reading. The instruments did more than Fraser's impassioned appeals to break down the Salish chief's resistance. He "consented to lend us his large canoe & to accompany us himself on the morrow."

Even the loan of one of the great dug-outs was better than continuing as uncertain passengers.

The morning of Saturday, July 2, 1808, began badly. A voyageur complained bitterly that his *sac à feu* had been stolen in the night, and the Indians refused to return it. Dogs had "dragged out and damaged many of our things." When Fraser asked the chief for the dug-out he thought the chief had agreed to loan, the chief seemed never to have heard about the request. He had presumably forgotten the promise made only a few hours previously.

Simon Fraser could stand no further delay. He had tried to make every reasonable offer in his power. Turning his back on the Salish chief, he stalked stubbornly down to the landing-place and ordered his voyageurs to float the heavy craft. The men eagerly took hold. Before they reached the water the chief yelled to his braves to stop them. Fraser ordered the voyageurs not to give way. For minutes the two groups struggled on the wet slippery shore, hauling the great dug-out forward and back. Fraser stood watching, stocky and determined, his hand longing to use the pistol his fingers caressed, while the Salish chief shouted that he was the greatest chief in the land, as powerful as the sun.

Simon Fraser could match the boast. His own canoe, cached back at Leon Creek, had not lightly been given its significant name, *Perseverance*, nor had the partners of the North West Company chosen this word as their motto without great qualities of determination and enterprise.

"As we could not go on without [it] we persisted and at last gained our point." In the great dug-out, accompanied by the chief and several of his braves, the party continued their journey until eleven o'clock. At eleven they were landed at a village where the natives shook hands but offered no further ceremony.

The owner of the dug-out was received with great warmth, and after much talk Fraser began to sense what lay behind the unusual lack of ceremony. These Indians living farther downstream than any he had met were trying to persuade the chief not to continue. They also tried to persuade Fraser not to go on. They talked with considerable passion and, a fact that slowly became apparent, with very real apprehension. They were afraid of the Musqueam, the coastal Indians who were their enemies. The Musqueam were very powerful. Not only would they destroy neighbouring Indians who trespassed on their lands, but every white man as well. Not unduly disturbed by their apprehensions and determined to impress them with his own strength, Fraser told them he was not afraid.

The announcement brought renewed protests. The Indians gathered round the dug-out and, perhaps afraid that it would be captured by the Musqueam, tried to haul it high on the shore. They begged the chief again and again not to go to the coast. They were so obviously terrified that their fear became infectious. To Fraser's surprise and dismay, the Little Fellow joined in the protests. He, too, was afraid of "the people at the sea."

Fraser told him to stay behind if he wanted to; the expedition could get on without him. Then, ignoring the Salish Indians' pleas and their efforts to haul the dug-out on shore, he ordered his men aboard. At last, with no one but his own party, he resumed his journey.

After two miles, in which time the *Canadien* voyageurs had an opportunity to accustom themselves to handling the great dug-out, "we came to a place where the river divides into several channels." Above the site of today's New Westminster, Fraser had to determine which channel to take. As the voyageurs slowed their pace while he pondered his decision, a canoe with several Salish Indians drew close. One of them volunteered to pilot the expedition into the right channel, and Fraser took him on board.

The guide directed the dug-out into the North Arm, and again Fraser made good time. But the good time was not fast enough to prevent several other smaller, swifter canoes from drawing close, and on them he recognized a number of braves from the Salish chief's village. As they came within a few canoe lengths the braves broke into a loud war-song, beating their paddles on the gunwales of their canoes, brandishing their bows and arrows and clubs and spears, and demanding the return of the dug-out.

It soon became apparent to Fraser that in the narrow North Arm they could readily overpower the white men in the heavy dug-out. He also knew that he could silence every one of his opponents by firing a single shot as he had longed to do at their village. But when he reached the Pacific he would have to return by the way he had come, if only to rescue the Little Fellow. He needed their co-operation.

He understood just how bad his situation had become when the Salish guide joined in the blood-chilling war chant and became "very unruly singing and dancing and kicking up the dust."

Fraser could smell the sea air. The tide ran tantalizingly high and strong. Thirty-six days and some five hundred miles from Fort George, he refused to let an unco-operative Indian endanger the lives of his men and the success of the expedition. Nor did it occur to him later to waste quill and ink and paper on the details by which he suppressed his hostile guide's violence.

"We threatened him with the effect of our displeasure and he was quiet."

Fraser also omitted to record the means by which he temporarily subdued the braves in their swift canoes. Such means were common knowledge to fur traders, winterers, and the partners and managing-directors in the head office in Montreal. This would not have been the first time he had relied on the force of his own courage to quell the activities of Indians. In his journal he dismissed the incident with a statement which, from another man and under other circumstances, might have been braggadocio: "This was an alarming crisis, but we were not discouraged: confident of our superiority, at least on the water, we continued."

A brief, terse entry recorded the greatest achievement of his lifetime: "At last we came in sight of a gulph or bay of the sea . . ."

Nine
The Longest Saturday

Fraser recorded . . . the results of his own tough and determined attempt to find a navigable route through the mountains to the sea. "The latitude is 49° nearly, while that of the entrance to the Columbia is 46°20′. This River, therefore, is not the Columbia."

"This the Indians call *Pas-hil-roe*. It runs in a S.W. & N.E. direction. In this bay are several high and rocky Islands whose summits are covered with snow."

Fraser had no time to write eloquent descriptions of what he saw and how he felt, no opportunity to remember, except perhaps fleetingly, that here was the goal of every North American explorer for hundreds of years—Columbus, Cartier, Hudson, La Vérendrye. Only twice before had white men reached the Pacific overland north of the Rio Grande—Mackenzie at Bella Coola in 1793, Clark and Lewis at the Columbia in 1805. Fraser was the third, and he fervently hoped that the river he had just descended was the Columbia.

It was a moment to make a man's scalp tingle and his gut tighten, to inspire a silent prayer of thanksgiving. There should have been a splendid celebration, with a tot of rum for every man who had helped to make the achievement possible—if Fraser had not broached the small half-keg when he had hoped the worst of the journey was past, a month ago at the *Portage du Baril*.

"On the right shore we noticed a village called by the Natives *Misquiame*; we directed our course towards it. Our turbulent passenger conducted us up a small winding river to a small lake to the village." No drums heralded Fraser's arrival at the Pacific. No Indians came running from the Musqueam village, on the low bench above the protected little inlet of the sea.

The Musqueam were considered much too hostile by the Salish for the neighbourly gesture of forwarding news of the strangers, as had happened often upstream. At the mouth of the river that he had followed all the way from Fort George, no one had ever heard of Simon Fraser except the men in his party.

He stepped ashore; his moccasins left their prints on the sloping silt the river had washed down for hundreds of miles. To his right the shore rose gradually to a tree-crested height a man could climb in half an hour, and beyond soared the mountains, peak after snow-crowned peak. To the left stretched the wide estuary, a far-reaching delta streaked with the low islands it had made, and more mountains very far in the distance. Ahead lay Fraser's great goal, the sparkling blue ocean, spaciously ornamented by rocky, tree-covered islands, the horizon a vague, broken line that might be more mountains or perhaps cloud banks shadowed by the late afternoon sun.

His men followed him ashore: two Fort George Indians who had come as guides and interpreters; nineteen *Canadien* voyageurs who had each paddled four thousand miles or more from Montreal; young Jules Quesnel, the son of a Quebec poet and musician; and John Stuart, born in Strathspey, Scotland, and due to rise to eminence in the fur trade (and to become uncle to the first Lord Strathcona). The men dallied only long enough to scoop up palmfuls of the water they expected to taste of salt; they were surprised to find it sweet, not knowing that the river was so strong that it merely forced its flow back on itself. Then, with Stuart and Quesnel, they hauled the heavy, loaded dug-out onto the silted shore, and took up their well-disciplined guard duty. Fraser climbed to the village, accompanied by the still-chastened Salish guide as a hostage, if a hostage might be needed, and several of the men. He longed for a better view of the ocean.

It was a view to make him forget the ordeal of the mountains, to want to stay for ever, to think and dream and wonder. But he did not linger long; he would come back for a much better look. Instead, he entered the gate of the stockaded Musqueam village "1500 feet in length and 90 feet in breadth." The village was ominously quiet. After minutes of calling out greetings dictated by the Salish guide, several old men and women crept out into the sunlight without a word or gesture of welcome. At Fraser's request one of them showed him round the numerous dwellings which were much like those of the Salish. Then they begged him to leave.

Fraser suspected that the Musqueam warriors had taken to the woods, possibly to observe the strangers whom they expected to fire on them, as earlier white mariners had done, or to be ready themselves to attack in strength.

Not knowing what to expect, he spent only an hour at the village. The scene he saw when he emerged from the stockade sent him racing to the shore.

During the hour the tide had ebbed. None of the party had had experience with tides, and all any of them had heard was wholly inadequate for coping with this phenomenon. Even Fraser could not know how far the tide would recede before it came in again, nor how long that would take.

"The tide had ebbed, and left our canoe on dry land."

The Salish dug-out was indeed an enticing target for the Musqueam. They sprinted from the trees in all directions, protecting themselves with their shields, "howling like so many wolves, and brandishing their war clubs."

While Fraser and the clerks whipped out their pistols, the voyageurs struggled to haul the cumbersome craft over the wet slippery shore until "at last we got into deep water, and embarked" with the Salish guide. The voyageurs paddled strongly and competently. Soon the white men were temporarily beyond danger of attack by the Musqueam. But not from the Salish braves who had waited out of sight to resume their pursuit.

Encouraged by the sight of his Salish friends drawing closer in their swift canoes, the guide also resumed his former hostility, demanding the white men's daggers and clothes and the packs. Fraser quickly put a stop to such demoralizing behaviour. "Being convinced of his unfriendly disposition, we turned him out and made him and the others, who were closing in upon us, understand that if they did not keep their distance we would fire upon them." Having made the trip by the North Arm, Fraser could find his way back; he was no longer desperately dependent on the services of any Indian guide.

"After this skirmish we continued until we came opposite the second village."

He longed to climb that inviting slope to yet another village overlooking the wide Pacific Ocean, to pause for a longer, more satisfying look at the panorama of water and islands and distant mountains, to ponder the way to the fabled ports of China.

That late afternoon, Fraser did not attempt a second landing. "Reflecting upon the reception we had experienced at the first, and the character of the Natives, it was thought neither prudent nor necessary to run any risk, particularly as we had no provisions, and saw no prospect of procuring any in that hostile quarter."

It had been a long day of continuous ordeals for his men and himself. Since the misty morning moment when the voyageur discovered that his pipe and tobacco were missing, through the struggle to procure the Salish chief's dug-out and to get it into the water, the decision as to which of the many channels to follow, the excitement of actually reaching the Pacific, and the attack by the Musqueam, none of them had eaten a morsel. There had been no opportunity to obtain food and no opportunity to eat. This was not the time to endanger the success of the expedition by foolhardiness. "We, therefore, turned our course and with the intention of going back to the friendly Indians for a supply, then to return and prosecute our design."

Tomorrow, Fraser would feast his eyes on the islands and mountains. Tomorrow, he would look joyously out over the ocean. Tomorrow, he might even climb one of those tall, straight trees to see farther, perhaps to study the extent of the river's jaundice-coloured incursion into the ocean's blue. Now he ordered his voyageurs to come about.

With the sun slanting over their shoulders, the men quickly picked up their paddle strokes. They were all, Fraser was sharply aware, tensed for further offence opposite the Musqueam village. He himself was not surprised to see that they would have to fight off not only the Musqueam but also the Salish waiting beyond.

"When we came opposite the hostile village the same fellows, who had annoyed us before, advanced to attack us which was echoed by those on shore. In this manner they approached so near that we were obliged to adopt a threatening position, and we had to push them off with the muzzles of our guns."

That day the threat of his guns saved Fraser, the Musqueam, like the Salish, having suffered at the hands of white men who had come in great ships and attacked their people with similar weapons. He had been saved from the need to fire the shots that would have ended the expedition and all news of it, except rumours such as those surviving the mariners' show of superior strength.

"The tide was now in our favour, the evening was fine, and we continued our course with great speed until 11, when we encamped within 6 miles of the Chief's village. The men being extremely tired, went to rest . . ." They were all together and all safe, so far. For that he was devoutly thankful. But he dared not let himself savour a moment of triumph until Stuart had determined their position.

At the end of that long Saturday, while the hungry voyageurs slept beside the great, borrowed dug-out and Stuart set up his instruments to determine the latitude by a star, Fraser waited in a torment of suspense. Ever since it broke from the mountains, the river had flowed in a much more westerly direction than its southerly course below Fort George. Since they had entered the North Channel, by the sun's position he thought it might have swung a little more to the north.

Fraser recorded Stuart's findings in a second terse journal entry, and with it the results of his own tough and determined attempt to find a navigable route through the mountains to the sea. "The latitude is 49° nearly, while that of the entrance to the

Columbia is 46°20′. This River, therefore, is not the Columbia."

Like his partner, Alexander Mackenzie, he had explored a river of disappointment. Like Mackenzie, he had not found the water route overland that his company needed. In the one remorseful moment he allowed himself, he observed bitterly: "If I had been convinced of this fact where I left my canoes, I would certainly have returned from thence."

That night he did not know whether he would ever see Leon Creek again.

Ten

"I Solemnly Swear . . ."

*One by one, they spoke the words: "I solemnly swear before
the Almighty God that I shall sooner perish than forsake
in distress any of our crew during the present voyage."*

"They were not long in bed before the tide rushed upon the beds and roused them up."

So began the first day of the return journey, long before dawn streaked the sky. While Fraser and Stuart had set up the instruments that confirmed their failure to find the Columbia, the weary, hungry voyageurs had unrolled their blankets beside the dug-out and had immediately fallen asleep. On a later trip they, or any man mad enough to repeat the ordeal, would know more about tides. Now they were learning the hardest way possible, by experience.

Half asleep, numbed with cold, the clothes they always slept in soaking wet, the men trailed their soggy blankets to higher ground and hauled up the canoe, all with no more light than the reflection of the sky off the water. There was no need for Fraser to announce formally the failure of the expedition. They could feel it in their bones. In their gloomy mood only one course could save them all from despair—action. As soon as the first light brightened the sky over the mountains, Fraser ordered the "*Lève! Lève! Nos gens . . . .*" Forced out of their surly discomfort, every man hurried to embark, eager to warm himself and dry his clothes with exercise.

They had camped about six miles from the Salish village where Fraser had commandeered the canoe, and where he hoped to obtain food. The voyageurs paddled against the current so desperately that they reached the village by five o'clock. Some of the Indians were already bathing in the river. Others came running at the sound of the noisy greetings, among them the Little Fellow.

The Hacamaugh's appearance did nothing to reassure Fraser or the voyageurs, nor did his recital of the treatment he had received during the twenty hours since the expedition had set out on the final lap to the sea. "He informed us that the Indians after our departure had fixed upon our destruction; that he himself was pillaged, his hands and feet tied, and that they had been about to knock him on the head" when one of the Salish from up the river had rescued him, and claimed him as a slave.

Securing the Little Fellow's release was easier than persuading the chief to feed the men who had forcibly borrowed his canoe. "We could not procure a morsel of provisions . . . and the Chief insisted upon having his canoe restored to him immediately." Again they and the Salish repeated yesterday's tug of war for the canoe and its precious contents. Faced with the dual danger of increased Indian hostility and his men's growing fears, Fraser turned on the now thoroughly hostile Indians. His voice sharp with the tension of the past few days, he roared at them, making "vehement gestures and signs exactly in their own way." For a moment they all fell back, quiet. But he knew that the truce would not last long.

It lasted long enough for him to come to a crucial, bitter decision. With no food, among hostile natives, his men hourly becoming more apprehensive, and with no hope of improving his situation, Simon Fraser gave up all thought of returning to the coast to take an observation for the longitude and for another look at the ocean; to return would mean suicide for himself and death, or worse, for his men. "But we could not proceed without the canoe, and we had to force it away from the owner leaving a blanket in its place."

The voyageurs were swinging into their stroke when he realized that one of them was missing. "The fellow being afraid had fled to the woods and placed himself behind a range of tombs." Returning for him wasted vital minutes, but Fraser did not hesitate. On this expedition no man would feel that he was not needed; no man would be left to face the wrath of the Indians alone.

"At last we got under way, and had to pull against a strong current."

The sight of the great dug-out pulling into the river again stung the Indians into pursuit in their smaller, swifter canoes. Knowing the white men could not now be trapped between their village and the ocean, they doubled their efforts, chanting their raucous war-songs and banging their paddles on the canoes as the voyageurs struggled to out-distance them. Again Fraser roared at them, this time threatening to shoot. Perhaps they shrewdly realized that he dared not risk shooting, for although they fell back they continued to follow. This time the truce was marred by three Indians who paddled out from a river on the left bank to investigate the strangers in the dug-out. They soon returned to the shore, but not before every man in Fraser's party had glimpsed the grisly human-scalp lock dangling on the chest of one of the warriors.

Fraser saw the pursuers land at dark. He kept his men paddling all through the night, hoping to get to the next village for food before they caught up. He reached his destination on a small island about eight o'clock, followed by the crafty Salish who had not made camp. They caught up as he landed. The chief at once demanded the return of the dug-out.

Seeing several canoes near by, Fraser agreed. He had his baggage piled on the shore, the greatly reduced packs of trade goods and all the personal equipment. Placing a guard under Quesnel and Stuart, he went to see about food. As soon as his back was turned several Salish rushed for the dug-out while others grabbed several packs. They stopped immediately when he came running at his men's yell for help. But the danger was not over. The Salish and the warriors from the local village crowded round in a great circle, every one armed with a spear or one of their great horn-clubs, all howling their blood-chilling war cries. "It was then, that our situation might really be considered as critical. Placed upon a small sandy Island, few in number, without canoes, without provisions, and surrounded by upwards of 700 barbarians. However our resolutions did not forsake us."

Fraser "applied for canoes in every direction, but could not procure any for love or money." He then appealed again to the Salish chief for the dug-out. "He asked his price—I consented—he augment his demand—I again yielded—he still continued to increase his imposition." Through sheer persistence and willpower Fraser eventually got the dug-out, though he also had to level his pistol at the Indians who tried to stop his men from loading the canoe. When the voyageurs at last pulled away, several were without paddles, and all lacked food.

The lack of food was almost as disastrous as the shortage of paddles and a leak in the dug-out. Not since leaving the Salish village on the morning of the second of July had any of them eaten. Late in the afternoon of the fourth, Fraser obtained a few fish, but not until the fifth—after four days and over a hundred miles of paddling—did they get a real meal of "five large Salmons." From the Indians who provided the salmon, he also obtained a paddle. The food and paddle staved off a despair even greater than that of the morning when the Pacific tide had swamped their camp because now the dug-out leaked so badly that every man was wet to his skin. That night Fraser and Stuart took turns on guard while the men slept, and across the river winked the menacing Salish camp-fires that warned against a daylight stop to repair the canoe.

As he kept his lonely, unhappy vigil, Fraser could now see the mountains silhouetted against the eastern sky and, to the west, the faintly glowing river twisting its broad way to the Pacific, the river that had relentlessly toughened the character of the Indians and that had more than once forced its will on him. But more than once his will had prevailed; and it would again.

Though he had been born in the New World, Simon Fraser boasted the blood of his Highland Scot forebears, the Lovat Frasers. After the Battle of Culloden, when his grandfather's mansion in Strathglass, Inverness-shire, had been burned by the Duke of Cumberland's men, his parents had overcome great hardships to make a living in the New World, where Simon was born in Vermont in 1776.

Of his father Simon knew only what his mother had told him, chiefly that he had died in prison for his stubborn loyalty to the British during the American revolutionary war. At times, much as he appreciated the schooling he had received in

Montreal through the kindness of his uncle Judge John Fraser, Simon had longed for the classical education his father had had. Now, on the melancholy return trip from the Pacific, he could not help but think of the fine books collected by his grandmother Margaret Macdonell of Glengarry, which had been confiscated by the American army. A knowledge of such books and a better education would have made the task of writing an account of his explorations much more worthy of the illustrious Lovat Frasers.

Perhaps he remembered his half-Indian children and the Métis girl he had married *au façon du nord* the previous winter; by this time she probably had a child. But his main concern that troubled night was for the men in his party, the voyageurs and Stuart and young Quesnel with his future still to make. And the Hacamaugh guide? With his heritage of wild Highland blood, Fraser could understand the aboriginal's distrust of unknown forces represented by the Musqueam and the Pacific.

In the morning the Salish were out early in their canoes; apparently they had been waiting for the dug-out. Hoping to escape them, Fraser took another channel. The pursuers followed, closing in swiftly. They came so close that Fraser and his clerks kept them from seizing the dug-out only by pushing them away with the muzzles of their guns. This time Fraser's loud commands failed to turn them back even momentarily or to force them to stay at a distance. Yelling fiercely, the Salish steadily manoeuvred the dug-out toward a rapids that would carry it downstream. For minutes the voyageurs kept clear. When it appeared that they might safely avoid the hazard, the Indians in the nearest canoe made a sudden powerful lunge with their paddles. The voyageurs saved the dug-out from swamping, but the thrust had swung them into the current. Paddling with all the strength of desperation and years of disciplined experience, they at last came to a spit of level shore. In a well-calculated swing they beached the dug-out at the foot of a high hill. Fraser immediately ordered Stuart and several men to disembark and cover the pursuing Indians while he and Quesnel got their arms and ammunition ready to run the blockade or to fight for their lives.

The Indians retired to the middle of the stream, to wait and watch. Assured that everything was in readiness, Fraser ordered the voyageurs who were on shore to embark. None obeyed. They had decided, Stuart reported, to go overland to the place where the party had camped on the twenty-fourth of June. The mountains were their only hope of survival. To continue to travel in the dug-out on the river, surrounded by hostile Indians watching every opportunity to attack and torment them, was worse than death.

Fraser looked from the little group of mutinous voyageurs to the Indians in their canoes. The voyageurs were men he had known for years and on whose loyalty and skill he depended. He knew their parents and his company would engage their younger brothers and their sons. They were his men and he was their *bourgeois*, and they were alone in hostile country, hundreds of miles from the nearest rude outpost of civilization. Above all, they were tired and they had eaten only one meal in five days.

To shoot or abandon the ring-leader of the voyageurs, if there was one, would be folly. Instead he himself landed to talk to them. With Stuart and Quesnel covering the canoes, he reminded them of the advantages of staying together, of the hopelessness of a small group of men surviving to find their unguided way through the mountains, of the obstacles along the way. With his back to the hill so he could see every move the Indians might make and every expression on the faces of the voyageurs, he talked about "our common welfare." Gradually as he saw their surly looks relax he offered his hand to each man in turn.

But that was not enough. A voyageur in acute distress could easily forget the clasping of paddle-hardened hands.

The nineteen voyageurs in the party had been brought up, as Fraser had been, in the Roman Catholic faith. Because of the circumstances of their life, few had been to confession since boyhood. But each, despite his outward roughness, remembered his home and his early training. Fraser now recalled that memory with all the reverence and superstition it evoked. Passionately, he prepared their mood for the oath he then imposed on each. In front of the two Fort George Indians and the Little Fellow, with the hostile Salish waiting in their canoes, he made each white man repeat that oath, alone before his fellows, and he repeated it himself. One by one, they spoke the words: "I solemnly swear before the Almighty God that I shall sooner perish than forsake in distress any of our crew during the present voyage."

That was the spiritual source of strength each man would need if he hoped to survive the days ahead. To it Fraser added a warmly reminiscent voyageur custom. Always, when a brigade of canoes neared its destination after a long trip, its leader called a brief halt so that every man could shave and put on his best shirt and cap and sash. Today there was no time for shaving, but the change of clothes evoked hopes of getting safely back to Fort George, surely in less than the forty-two days they had already spent on the trip so far.

The men tossed their ragged, filthy, discarded clothes into the river, and rolled up everything they had left into the customary packs. Even to reduce the weight of those packs that would have to be carried up and down the dreaded mountain trails lightened their spirits a little. The temporary repairs to the dug-out, made under the protection of Fraser's and the clerks' pistols, cheered every man further. But it was the reverent, dedicated ceremony that really made the difference in their outlook.

By the time they had the dug-out safe to float again, every voyageur willingly embarked. Still covering their departure with the weapons against which the Salish had no effective defence, Fraser could now risk firing—if firing became absolutely necessary. "Full of spirits, singing and making a great noise," the voyageurs paddled boldly past the lurking canoes. Not a shot was fired. That strange singing and the magic of the white men's renewed *esprit de corps* had won the mingled respect and fear of the proud Indians of the great river valley. One by one, they turned their canoes about and paddled back to their villages.

Well after sunset, Fraser ordered camp to be made on a small island below the "bad rock," between the modern towns of Hope and Yale.

Eleven
Hell's Gate Again

Looking up to dizzying heights at length after length of pole ladders lashed together with bark rope, Fraser's own gut tightened. But for the example he must set his men he might not have been able to grasp the first rung and heave himself up rung after rung till he feared he could go no farther.

*N*o explorer knew better than Fraser that going up a river is harder than going down.

The worst thing about going up Fraser's river in that July 1808 was the knowledge that it was not the Columbia. Gone was the buoying hope that they were on the river they had set out to explore. Nothing remained to keep them struggling on except their sorely tested determination to get back to Fort George, and even that quailed before the prospect of the canyon.

Coming upstream from the Pacific, Fraser had seen how the river had broken its way out of the mountains. It had burst into the valley as though it, too, thanked God for being free of those savage, confining rocks which had held it prisoner for so many miles. It exulted in the broad, beautiful valley it had made, caring nothing for a little party of men from far away who wanted to use it for their own convenience and profit.

For the first few days after escaping his Salish pursuers, Fraser blamed them for frustrating his plan to determine the longitude at Musqueam and to explore the great estuary. But for them, he felt certain, his men might have been willing to stay for a few days, or even weeks.

His bitter resentment persisted as he toiled up the rough trail past Lady Franklin Rock into the canyon itself to a portage where he met a small band of Indians who had camped to fish. These Indians were friendly. Their old men talked eagerly with the white strangers. On learning from the Little Fellow that the strangers had been to the ocean, they wanted to know all about the fabulously powerful coastal people. Delighted with his attentive audience, the Little Fellow proudly recounted stories of Fraser's remarkable exploits, how he had survived attack after attack, how effective were his big guns which he merely aimed at his enemies to subdue them and, boasted the Hacamaugh guide, the white men's pockets were full of similar little guns.

The scene was one that had occurred scores of times on the upper stretches of the trip, a small band of natives awed by the known or imagined powers of white men. But after the resistance he had encountered from the Salish, he could no longer regard Indians as mere simple people casting their nets for fish beside the river's edge. He had to stress his superiority by firing several shots. He was similarly suspicious of the next band they overtook, whose young men helped the voyageurs on the portage. On learning that two or three items had been pilfered from the packs, instead of ignoring the incident as an ancient Indian prerogative, he announced sharply that if he could lay his hand on the culprit that Indian would have "reason to regret his rapacity." In his journal he reminded himself that "this was a lesson not to be forgotten during the remainder of the Journey."

But gradually his good judgment and experience restored his sense of perspective with the chance help of two local Hacamaugh chiefs. The chiefs were so pleased to see him again that they immediately loaned him their two small canoes and went on foot to the next village. Their casual, generous act reminded Fraser of one fact he had known all along: the river, and not the Indians, was his real adversary. It was the river, suddenly unrestrained and bountiful as it flowed down its wide valley, that had shaped the character of the Salish. Indians living in the harsh, hostile canyon environment had been forced through the centuries to become tough and athletic, willing to help strangers and friendly.

At the "bad rock" Fraser and every man in his party, except perhaps the Little Fellow, had realized that for most of the return journey to Fort George they would be struggling against the river's current. "At the end of navigation" they had to abandon the now useless dug-out that had made possible that brief glimpse of the Pacific, and had caused so much trouble. Fraser presented the dug-out and a few other articles not easily carried to the Little Fellow who gleefully shared them with his Indian friends. Then "each of us took charge of his own bundle."

With their greatly reduced baggage, they trudged on until they met the two Hacamaugh chiefs, who not only loaned their canoes, but "they gave us plenty to eat, and entertained us with a variety of songs, dances, &c., during the evening."

The Indians' co-operation so relieved the prolonged strain that Fraser paused for an entire morning while "we dried our things." Drying clothes and yards of faded calico on bushes on a sunny morning not only reminded every man of a familiar sight on other long canoe trips, but on that fine July day the custom served to provide a much needed break before the ordeal of the canyon.

Their stop at the next village, a few miles distant, was equally reviving. By that time news of the expedition had already spread so far that "we met with much attention." The Indians gave the voyageurs a present of two of those "excellent dogs which made delicious meals." But the highlight of the stop was an opportunity to procure "a few articles of curiosity." Like all travellers Fraser and his men wanted souvenirs of their trip, though the souvenirs had to be things they needed or could easily carry; among several articles, they took away a blanket made of dog's hair, a "matted bag," and a wooden comb "of curious construction." They also took with them memories of one special "curiosity" not for barter, a bunch of brass keys. The brass keys, the Indians said, had come from the crew of a ship destroyed by coastal Indians several years before. Those grim souvenirs were not easily forgotten by the white men. Had they belonged to one of the Spaniards' ships, to the Russians, to an American or a British captain whose fate they themselves might have escaped?

After the little break for rest and diversion Fraser set out early in the morning with several local Hacamaugh as guides. Ahead stretched the Black Canyon and Hell's Gate.

"The road was inconceivably bad," he recorded. He had no words adequate to describe that aboriginal trail up and down treacherous rocks and defiles and precipices. On the return trip it seemed even worse than going down. Looking up to dizzying heights at length after length of pole ladders lashed together with bark rope, Fraser's own gut tightened. But for the example he must set his men he might not have been able to grasp the first rung and heave himself up rung after rung till he feared he could go no farther. Fresh terror seized him with every chance gust of wind that swung the tenuous length of ladder out from the rock face and sickeningly back against it. And never were the rungs the same distance apart or of the same width. While his hands gripped the rung above his head, he had to feel with his feet for one below, not daring to risk a look that might take his eyes down to the river. Nor was that the worst part of the ordeal. "The most perilous was, when another rock projected over the one you were leaving."

But no, even more terrifying was going down those free-swinging ladders fifty times a man's height, and more. Descending, a man could not resist looking down. He could only trust that the ladder up which Indians had been travelling for years, for centuries perhaps, would not give way. Descending some of the pole ladders, Fraser had to entrust even his gun to a native. The terrified voyageurs, as they had been on the trip to the ocean, were temporarily a grave liability. They could not carry packs up and down and across the canyon wall. Fraser and his clerks had to plead with them to continue until they themselves had used every effort of nerve and reassurance they could command. Never had he had greater need to depend on the natives or to marvel at the ease with which they climbed "these wild places with the same agility as sailors do on board of a ship."

That night, when every white man had at last reached comparative safety for the time being, the Indians provided a meal of dried salmon.

In the morning, after a brief, easy trek, the party reached a stretch of water that was obviously navigable since Fraser found three canoes on the beach.

They appeared like manna, those canoes. They were a miracle to voyageurs too weak to continue without a long rest, and Fraser commandeered them without qualm. "Those that were lame embarked," recorded the explorer; "the others continued by land." Some on the river struggling up against the strong current, others following the ancient trail, the expedition continued throughout the day. When they reached the village where they had camped on that unforgettable twenty-fourth of June, they were again fed, and in the morning canoes were again provided for the men who were too lame to walk. Without such assistance, Fraser would not have known what to do with the poor wretches whom he would not leave behind. Without the co-operation of successive bands of Hacamaugh he could never have persuaded and cajoled and threatened his men to continue till they overcame the second worst stretch of the canyon, Hell's Gate, nor to go on to face the approach to Jackass Mountain.

In the confusion at the beginning of the portage below Jackass Mountain, where the lame voyageurs would have to be assisted to climb the narrow trail across the rock slide, Jules Quesnel lost his way. For hours he was missing. While several voyageurs went in search, accompanied by a party of Indians, the others waited and the July heat steadily mounted. The forced rest was good for the lame voyageurs. It almost drove Fraser mad. Hour after hour passed in an agony of anxiety: what if they had to search for days? What if they never found Quesnel, fallen, perhaps, down a bottomless chasm? Usually stoical and resourceful, that day he did not know what to do. Fortunately, the young clerk found his way back before dark.

With a very early start the entire party crossed the hazardous stretch along the face of the rock slide before a torrential rain storm broke the heat wave.

Every voyageur had dreaded this place, without the added terror of a severe mountain storm. It was here that they had tried to run the rapids on their own, here D'Alaire had miraculously escaped death by riding the maelstrom on the broken half of an upturned canoe. Here was the trail where they had watched one of their fellows save his life by grabbing a jutting rock, and where the kettle had broken loose from his pack and had bounced into the river. Now as they huddled together, thunder crashed like cannonfire between the echoing heights, and lightning knifed menacingly through the angry clouds. When the storm eventually abated, every garment they wore was soaked and every man was shivering, whether from the sudden chill air or from fear he could not have said. Perhaps because it reminded them of their brush with tragedy on the trip down, perhaps in a mood of surly discomfort, they refused to camp at the site chosen by their *bourgeois*.

"Such conduct under the circumstances in which we were, was unpleasant," Fraser commented in a burst of bitter understatement, adding tartly: "Lost some time waiting for the men who thought proper to remain behind." But, after a reprimand, he accepted their excuse that their bad conduct was due to the weather. He, too, was wet and chilled. He may even have shared their superstitious fear that the place was evil.

On the morning of July 14, *bourgeois*, clerks, and voyageurs rejoiced to find themselves above the rapids "where we escaped perishing the 20th June." In their newly achieved, comparative safety they turned an incident that might have been a sombre reminder of that day into a brief celebration: two guides who had helped on the way down appeared with several articles they had retrieved after the canoes had been swamped. Among them was a cap and a pair of moccasins, articles to be treasured by the owners who claimed them amid excited congratulations.

A few hours later Fraser reached the forks of the Thompson. Despite hardships none could have imagined, they had all survived a second canyon passage, and they had made the return trip in a week, practically the same time as going down.

The Hacamaugh chief and his warriors were waiting. So was a tribe from the interior, who spoke a strange language and rode fine horses. The horses reminded Fraser of the old Tauten chief's repeated advice to travel overland.

He still had enough trade goods to barter for horses for himself and Stuart and Quesnel, leaving the voyageurs to make their own way to Fort George. Travelling light, he would be more likely to reach the post in good time to get news of his exploration to Fort Chipewyan before winter set in.

Fraser did not barter for the horses. He had not forgotten the oath sworn beside the surging river in the presence of the watchful Salish, nor that the men made lame on the journey would need firm, considerate care if they were to recover for further duty. Above all, he wanted to take a second look at every mile of the river, especially the navigable miles.

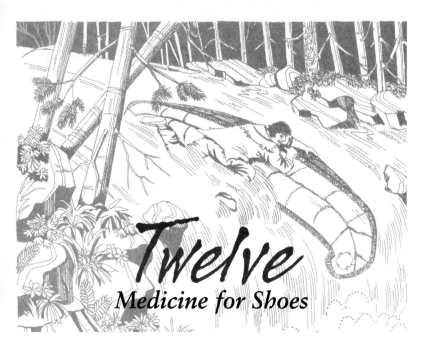

Twelve
Medicine for Shoes

A couple of days later, when the weather was again very bad, the Lillooet chief gave Fraser the most welcome gift in the world, a roll of tough, well tanned and greased blacktail-deer moccasin-leather: "Continually walking as we were among the worst of roads, our feet were covered with blisters."

*B*efore leaving the Thompson, Fraser checked the expedition's finances: how much trade goods did he have left to barter on their way back to Fort George? Or until they reached the cache at Leon Creek, if the cache remained intact? It was five or six days distant, at least.

He had spent more than he could well afford in the valley trying to curry favour among the various Salish tribes, and even among the friendly Hacamaugh in the canyon. Many packs had been lost. Most of his calico gowns were gone, which were a prime favourite with the chiefs. The heavy goods such as ironware, of which he had had very little, had been left at Leon Creek or exchanged long ago to lighten the cargo. He had no rum at all, though the lack of rum was not a serious handicap because the Indians on this river were not yet accustomed to it. In fact, his entire available resources at the Thompson were several packs of small commodities—awls and knives, beads and other trinkets—fortunately the most wanted items in the mountains where commerce with the coast was so difficult and trade with the tributary Thompson still undeveloped. Within a few years, if Fraser survived to send his reports east to Montreal, the North West Company would accustom the Indians on both rivers to many commodities for which they could be persuaded to provide services and to trap valuable furs.

However, foreseeing future trade would not help him at the moment. His immediate problem was to find some means of stretching his resources. The situation would have been easier if none of the voyageurs had become lame. Men who were able to walk—and he still was, thank God!—could survive without canoes, even though they made poor time. For those who could not walk more than short distances and who would not be able to do so for many days, he absolutely must have canoes. He must have food too. And help to carry the packs. Guides he no longer urgently needed, for he had now travelled the river once.

It was not enough for Fraser to spend his currency only for such obvious services as canoes and food and portaging. Old hand that he was as explorer–fur trader, he could calculate to the last bright bead the price he must pay for goodwill. Here good-will was a prime necessity. It stood for prestige, and prestige among Indians as affluent as those with access to the Thompson country was at least half the price of safety. Lack of it would surely become news that would spread from band to band as swiftly as the river flowed below the Hacamaugh village.

A solution for his worst financial difficulties had occurred to him a month ago: below the Lillooet village, on the trail he would soon be plodding again, he had obtained a canoe from a sick Indian in exchange for some medicine. He still had a few medicaments which, though they had cost very little in Montreal, here were practically priceless.

Leaving Quesnel and the men at the riverside with the packs, he and Stuart climbed the high bank to the Hacamaugh village and the camps of the various visiting tribes from the interior, where the Indians were waiting to begin the usual ceremonies.

After smoking the calumet, enjoying a meal, and watching the Indians dance, Fraser accepted the gift of an otter belt. Then he presented his own carefully considered gifts in return, the absolute minimum calculated to continue the Indians' respect and enthusiasm for his person and his cause. He shook hands with hundreds of braves. For a few brief hours he savoured his role. He enjoyed the colourful pageant with the mountains as a backdrop, the summer dwellings, the horses grazing, here and there a green horse-hide hanging on a tree. But it was the Indians themselves who mattered, particularly the strangers from up the Thompson: "Crowding round they gazed on us with astonishment."

The brief, ceremonial visit laid the foundations for future trade. It also provided Simon Fraser with the means whereby he could reinforce his prestige and at the same time improve his finances through a service for the natives.

At the beginning of the nineteenth century even civilized people believed that a priest or a doctor or the king possessed some rare magic by which they could heal the sick: the king's touch was greatly prized in Europe. At the confluence of the Thompson and the Fraser River that July afternoon in 1808, the explorer attempted the ancient art of the healing touch.

Throughout the camps he saw many children suffering from the effects of an epidemic which "reduced them to skeletons." Several were brought to him by their neatly dressed, distraught mothers who begged for medicine. Fraser could find no reason to disappoint either the mothers or the children. He was not a doctor. He was, however, a fur trader who for many years had had to depend on his own resources in treating himself and his men. Hoping he still had some Turlington, a popular remedy of the day, among his simple medicaments, he sent Stuart for a vial.

However, Stuart returned without the Turlington. It was all gone. Instead he brought some laudanum.

"Considering the one of equal value with the other towards a cure, I mixed a few drops of what he brought with water. In this mixture I dipt my finger which I gently applied to the forehead of the sick. Believing no doubt in miracles, within a few minutes, there were upwards of four score applicants for a touch of my finger; and had we remained any length of time, I have reason to believe the whole camp, which exceeded 1200, would have followed the example."

To the Indians living in the vicinity of the Thompson and Fraser rivers, the shrewd, kindly act became a momentous occasion, long to be talked about. Whether they actually believed in miracles or whether experience had taught them to doubt such wonders, for the explorer the gentle touch of his finger dipped in water and a few drops of laudanum guaranteed their friendly co-operation. Though he would continue to pay a fair price for their services, they would be eager to see him. Along the river he was travelling they would all know about him and compete for his attention.

When he set out again he had canoes for the men who needed them. At the next village, the Indians "regaled us with Dog's flesh." A couple of days later, when the weather was again very bad, the Lillooet chief gave Fraser the most welcome gift in the world, a roll of tough, well tanned and greased blacktail-deer moccasin-leather: "Continually walking as we were among the worst of roads, our feet were covered with blisters." Some of the men who were lame were in perpetual torture. From the hides the voyageurs, with the willing help of local Indian women, quickly stitched new footwear.

That day Fraser met again the ailing Indian who, a month before, had bartered his canoe for medicine. He was "still there and unwell," but still apparently hopeful that he could be restored to good health. Another sick Lillooet begged Fraser to give him some medicine in exchange for a pair of moccasins. And, all along the difficult stretch between the Thompson and the main Lillooet village, canoes were available wherever they could be used. At the village the Lillooet provided ample food with a special treat for the voyageurs, another feast of wild dogs.

Four days after leaving the Thompson, Fraser camped a day's travel below Leon Creek and sent the Little Fellow to the nearest Indians for provisions. The Hacamaugh brought back salmon, and the shocking news that "the greatest part of the *cache*" had been destroyed by wild animals; that what remained had been saved through the constant attention of the Indians left in charge—services for which Fraser suspected he might have to pay.

The news plunged the voyageurs back into their gloomy mood. For days they had hoped that the worst was past. Now they remembered the hardships of the valley and the canyon. They talked about starving to death. A few suggested they had better stay with the natives. One man actually remained behind his fellows for a time with an Indian band, though he hurried to catch up when he realized that the others were all going on. Even the meeting with a small band of Atnah, old friends on the journey, was marred by the Atnah's news that a large party of Indians was travelling on the trail high above a rapids where

Fraser had had considerable difficulty on the way down.

Fraser did not share his voyageurs' excited apprehension that the Indians on the trail would surely hurl rocks down on the little party, though he prudently decided to post an extra sentry. Knowing that a small party of armed white men could ensure their safe passage at the rapids, his real concern was for the cache, or what remained of it, now almost within sight. Whatever remained would help them to reach Fort George. A few scraps of iron and half a dozen awls and knives would provide bales of dried salmon, if the salmon stored on the scaffolds was all gone. A single copper kettle could be bartered for canoes, if the cherished birch-bark craft had all been completely broken.

Since it was now too late in the day for the entire party to reach the site of the cache before dark, Fraser camped and sent Stuart and two of the strongest voyageurs ahead to guard the cache.

In the morning he set out at first light. Travelling as fast as his weakened men could walk or be paddled, he caught his first glimpse of the scaffold a few hours later as he rounded a bend. It looked intact. He soon saw that it was in fact intact. Stuart and the voyageurs were waving excitedly, yelling words he could not yet hear above the roar of Leon Creek. But they were good, reassuring words. That he knew from his friend's eloquent gestures. "We had the inexpressible satisfaction of finding our canoes and our *cache* perfectly safe." The rumours heard by the Little Fellow at the Indian village proved to be completely false. Fraser had no further need to buy shoes with medicine.

The Indians left in charge had taken good care of the packs buried in the ground and the canoes on the scaffolds. The bales of dried salmon were untouched, and Fraser had goods with which to pay for the loyal service. Mercurially happy again, the voyageurs lowered the familiar birch-bark canoes and set about making repairs. The most surly and lame among them eagerly assisted wherever he could. While the Little Fellow and the Atnah went on to the next portage, Fraser, once again aboard the *Perseverance*, left Leon Creek with his entire party.

"At 3 P.M. all being ready we took our departure. Safe in our canoes we had reason to consider ourselves as once more at home, and notwithstanding the many disagreeable moments which we had experienced, we talked of them as nothing and we felt happy. Encamped at dark."

Thirteen

"Our Cache Perfectly Safe"

With the threat of starvation lessening with every
cache Fraser found intact . . . the bales of dried salmon
enabled him to reward handsomely the Indians who had
guarded the caches, especially those who themselves
were hungry as they awaited the salmon run.

"*Je suis un homme du nord!*" That was the proud boast of every voyageur who crossed the height of land west of Lake Superior. He had received the coveted designation at a special ceremony above the *grand portage*. It set him apart from his fellows, the pork-eaters who had paddled only from Montreal to the depot. Some day, if the *Canadiens* continued to open further river-roads linking the east with the Pacific Coast, they might evolve a ceremony worthy of their special exploits. Until that happened Fraser's voyageurs were still northmen, but nineteen unique northmen who had paddled farther than any others in the world.

Now, just to be back in the familiar birch-bark canoes improved their morale and eased their tortured feet and aching back muscles.

Soon they would be out of these overpowering, inhospitable, snow-peaked mountains. They were again sure of having two meals every day. What did it matter that the current was so strong, that they had to paddle uphill all the way to Fort George? Settling themselves in the accustomed positions, grasping their familiar paddles, every man felt that some day, please God, he would sing again.

But not yet.

"We had to oppose a strong current, and encountered great difficulties in the rapids."

Next day they were soaked by driving rain. A strong wind

made the canoes difficult to manage. Because the spring run-off had ended, the river level had dropped considerably, creating more carrying places than on the trip down. At the *Rapide Couvert*, which they reached a couple of days after recovering the cache, they had to carry everything over the entire mile of rocky, precipitous hills. By the time the voyageurs had trudged that mile and returned for more packs, some of their cheer had waned. They would need more than a few days to regain their usual physical stamina and their habitual cheery spirits.

Even Fraser would need time to recover his energy and sense of values. At the end of the long, arduous portage, he met more Atnah friends, among them the old chief, who was delighted to see him. Fraser petulantly confided to his journal that the Atnah "annoyed us with their caresses." He could not force himself to answer all their eager questions about the trip. The old chief said he and his people had been very anxious about the white men, and would have gone to avenge their deaths if "the Indians of the sea" had destroyed them. Fraser replied with a curt retort: much as he appreciated their friendship and good intentions, they must understand that he and his men by "our nature and our arms were superior to any thing we could meet among the Indians."

He was still slightly suspicious of every native he met, despite continued proof to the contrary. But gradually, as he recovered, his better judgment returned.

He laughed with his men at the sight of a tiny, strangely designed pine-bark canoe with narrow bows pointing downward like a funnel. "*Un canot puit au bec d'Eturgeons!*" someone cried delightedly, as they watched it cross the river with its capacity load of two persons. "A sturgeon-nosed canoe!"

Having tartly reminded these old friends of his pre-eminence, Fraser accepted their hospitality and their gifts; he was specially pleased to receive a generous bundle of moccasin leather. Later, as good Indian manners dictated, he presented his Atnah hosts with gifts of equal or better value.

The end of the *Rapide Couvert* portage was also the end of his association with the Hacamaugh guide who had served the expedition so well. The Little Fellow was willing to go with Fraser all the way to Fort George, but his Indian friends advised him to return to his own people. Fraser let him choose his own presents, articles "such as pleased him most," and parted with a man whose knowledge of his people and the Fraser River country had contributed materially to the safety of every man as well as to the success of much of the trip.

For almost a week, until they were completely out of the mountains, the old chief and his young men travelled a strange course with Fraser. The white men continued in their canoes, struggling up portages—at the *portage du Baril* the weather was so hot that the trail seemed even longer than on the trip down—hauling the craft in low water, making good time on increasingly frequent smooth stretches. Meanwhile, the Indians rode their horses across country. Each night the two groups met and often the Atnah brought gifts of food. One evening they appeared with a great treat, a "plentiful feast made up of venison, onions, Roots &c." Except for a few wild dogs, the venison was the first fresh meat the white men had eaten in two months. One of the guides shot a deer the same day. With the threat of starvation lessening with every cache Fraser found intact, the fresh meat became a luxury. It and the bales of dried salmon enabled him to reward handsomely the Indians who had guarded the caches, especially those who themselves were hungry as they awaited the salmon run. Being in a position to reward deserving Indians pleased Simon Fraser greatly; it was also good business.

Near Soda Creek Canyon, the old Atnah chief announced that the pleasant evening meetings were at an end. He was back in his own country, and he must stay with his people. It was a cordial but sad parting between two men who had come to respect one another's courage and enterprise. As a token of their mutual respect, and of his own debt, Fraser made a suitable speech and presented the old chief with a gun and some ammunition. To the chief's brother who had loyally guarded the large cache of dried salmon, he gave a "Poniard." He also promised to come back or to send one of his partners to build a trading-post in the vicinity.

Now, though occasional groups of Indians might dash up to the camp-sites on horses and in war-paint, and more portages and rapids had to be overcome, the worst dangers were truly past. Voyageurs who had been too lame to walk were well again. Occasionally, trying out their voices, they sang on open stretches of river after they had enjoyed a "pipe." Above the Quesnel River where they felt almost at home, they recalled songs long forgotten. There, between steep clay-banks where, until the party paddled downstream two months before, a gay French chanson had never been heard, now La Vérendrye's *Malbrouck* echoed and the lovely, nostalgic *A la claire fontaine*:

At the clear fountain
As I walked by,
The beautiful water
Said, come bathe in me.
Long have I loved you,
Ne'er forgot will you be.

Reminded by the songs of home and the far-off St. Lawrence, the voyageurs sang oftener and sometimes tenderly. It was not so with Simon Fraser, the explorer.

What had he to sing about? How could French love-songs or Scottish laments relieve his ever-increasing awareness of failure? What could the wild roses and the wild onions at the West Road River mean to him except to remind him that here Alexander Mackenzie had set off overland to complete his trip across the continent?

They had much in common, Fraser and Mackenzie. Each had discovered his River of Disappointment, great streams which, though adding enormously to the known geography of the North American continent and to British territory, were useless as canoe highways. Each had a Highland Scottish background, and had received at least part of his education in Montreal. Each had crossed the continent several times. Each was a competent fur trader. But Mackenzie, born twelve years before Fraser, had not only explored a great, seemingly useless river, he had been the first white man to cross the continent north of the Rio Grande. That fact gave him special prestige. He had also published in London the account of his voyages which had been a great success and had brought him to the attention of George III by whom he had been knighted. He was now famous on both continents, living in great comfort in London. Very great comfort, it seemed, compared with the trip Fraser was now completing.

Fraser, also, hoped to publish a book about his explorations. But remembering his grandmother's great interest in literature and his father's sound classical education he felt himself inadequate for such a task. During his first year in New Caledonia he had become so uncomfortable with a quill and ink that he had sent his journal to John Stuart with a note that revealed his keen sense of frustration: "It is exceeding ill wrote worse worded & not well spelt. But there I know you can make a good Journal of it, if you expunge some Parts & add to others and make it out in the manner you think most Proper. It will make away with a good deal of your time and Paper but I think it necessary to send it to headquarters in the light canoe as it will give our Gentlemen a good deal of information about the Country."

He could not have known, as he brooded in the *Perseverance* during the last days before reaching Fort George, that Sir Alexander Mackenzie had written similarly to his cousin Roderick Mackenzie in the winter of 1789–90 after his trip to the Arctic. Nor that the polished phrases of Mackenzie's now famous *Voyages* had been ghost-written by William Combe, the learned author of *The Tours of Dr. Syntax*, in a London debtor's prison.

But in all their common problems as explorers, nothing could have inspired greater rapport between himself and Mackenzie during the first few days of August than the slowness of early-nineteenth-century communication. Months would pass before Fraser would be able to share his news with the other winterers at Fort Chipewyan, far down the Peace. Not until next July and the company's annual meeting would he be able to give the majority of his partners a full account of his exploration of the river that was not the Columbia. For that satisfaction he must nurse his thoughts for a full year, until he reached Fort Kaministiquia, the depot recently renamed Fort William in honour of William McGillivray, chief director of the North West Company.

The awareness of that slow, gnawing, inevitable distance in time and space sobered Fraser's joy of homecoming as his voyageurs swept up to the tiny log Fort George at noon on Sunday, August 6, 1808, "where we found Mr. Faries with his two men."

What could he, Simon Fraser, say to the young clerk, Faries, that would seem to justify the time and effort and expense of the exploration of the Fraser River?

Fourteen

"Nothing to Reproach Ourselves with"

. . . "This journey did not meet the needs of the Company and will never be of any advantage to them, this river not being navigable, but we have nothing to reproach ourselves with, having done what we set out to do."

*F*raser's achievement in bringing his entire party safely back to Fort George was a triumph of leadership and courage. Together they had travelled more than a thousand miles of uncharted territory, almost all of it never before seen by white men. They had explored the most savage river on the continent. They had made history, though that fact might mean little to the nineteen voyageurs. When the time came to yarn before the kitchen fires back east they would boast above all that they were now more than northmen; they had been to the Pacific Ocean, the fabulous *mer de l'ouest*, the goal of the earliest French explorer.

John Stuart and Jules Quesnel could also share in the boast, and young Quesnel did so in a letter to a friend in Montreal. Quesnel described the two-months-long ordeal, the "appalling mountains that we could never have crossed if the natives, who received us well, had not helped us," and their disappointment upon discovering that the river was not the Columbia. Then, at the end of his letter, he summed up their situation: "This journey did not meet the needs of the Company and will never be of any advantage to them, this river not being navigable, but we have nothing to reproach ourselves with, having done what we set out to do."

The young clerk might have been speaking for his *bourgeois*; perhaps he had heard Fraser use those very words. Though the exploration of the Fraser River was a herculean achievement, it was just another river explored by a Nor'Wester in the course of his life as a fur trader. Nor'Westers had been exploring rivers ever since the original partners signed their first casual agreement in 1779. With every river the cost of transport increased. Every river explored in the dual search for more furs and for an overland route that would keep the company solvent increased costs. This would be so until a river that could be used for canoes was discovered on the long Pacific slope.

During most of the journey to the sea and all the way back, the cost of the expedition had worried Fraser. It was as if the fate that had haunted his family for generations had crossed the Atlantic and the entire North American continent with him. Probably it was the kind of fate he had been brought up to expect, his parents and his ancestors having been born and raised not far from Macbeth's Cawdor Castle and practically in sight of the ancient Witches' Cave. In Inverness-shire, along the east shore of Loch Ness, the Highlanders had known little but trouble even before the English came in 1715. Trouble and struggle had always been Simon Fraser's companions.

As it was with every other young man in the North West Company, every pound he owned was tied up in his partnership, and he knew that he was fortunate to have the connection, so hard were times during the war with France. But what hope had he now of helping his widowed mother, of setting himself up for eventual retirement to a more comfortable life? And the failure of the expedition affected the hopes of every other wintering partner. Every man's income would suffer because of the cost of this abortive exploration.

He had had approximately one canoe load of trade goods with which to finance his trip. The contents of a north canoe, most of it imported from England, was valued at £375 at Fort William. The cost would be increased at least two hundred times by the time the goods reached the Pacific—the mark-up on shot and ball was 400 per cent at Fort Chipewyan and on high wines 350 per cent—calculated partly on the wages for the two clerks, the nineteen voyageurs, and the two Indian guide-interpreters. In the Athabasca Department clerks received £100 a year; a *bout* or bowman, and steersman, 600 livres or about £30; and middlemen a little less; all plus equipment. Generally, the men lived off the country during the winter months, but had to be fed on canoe trips when they had no time to fish or hunt. In well-established fur-trade departments these costs would be met by the sale of furs trapped by the Indians. New Caledonia was still an undeveloped area where the expenses would continue to pile up for two or three or more years, with practically no income.

What would the partners have to say about the cost of the trip at the annual meeting of the North West Company at Fort William—those tough, shrewd, enterprising men battling wartime restrictions, ever increasing costs, and the Hudson's Bay Company, Astor, the American government, and the Russians?

Would history consider the trip worth the cost in money and human effort? Would future generations profit from their losses? Or would the brave, perilous journey never be remembered?

Fraser resumed the routine of the fur trade when he got back to Fort George. After planning the winter's trapping with Stuart, and the middle-Fraser and Nechako Indians, he left on a great round-about trip to Fort Chipewyan. He hoped to reach the headquarters of the Athabasca Department before freeze-up. Whether he got there by canoe or had to complete the trip on snowshoes, he intended to visit each of the new posts in the vast area of the Upper Fraser and the Parsnip and Peace rivers. His great aim was to make New Caledonia pay its way as quickly as possible. The success or failure of that aim depended largely on the morale and physical toughness of the few white men, probably not more than a half dozen, living in rude, widely separated posts at the uttermost end of civilized communication. Because he was short of trade goods, Fraser made the most of a good talk with each of these isolated clerks—all in their late teens or early twenties—about the virtues of duty and courage and hard work.

Often he had time for brooding and reflection as he sat for long hours in the *Perseverance*. He knew what he had accomplished. He knew he had made a great contribution to the search for an overland link between Montreal and the Pacific Ocean. He had added very significant, if negative, information. Henceforth every explorer would know that Fraser's river was not the Columbia. It was not the most cheering knowledge for the explorer of that river, but it meant that other men would be spared his ordeal.

Rested and gradually recovered from the rigours of his trip to the Pacific, Fraser's good sense assured him that more than negative information would accrue from his exploration. David Thompson might even now have found and travelled the entire Columbia; if only there was a means of communicating with him instead of being, in effect, as far apart as opposite ends of the earth! When Thompson or some other man explored the Columbia, some use would be made of the middle and upper Fraser. Despite its savage mountain passages, his river was partially navigable; this he had proved.

But there was a much more significant aspect to this summer's achievement. North West Company partners might rail, with good reason, about the cost of exploring a river that was useless for cross-continent travel; none could overlook its political importance. Through the posts he had established in preparation for the trip and the trip itself to the Straits of Georgia, Fraser had acquired many thousands of square miles of territory to which Great Britain could lay claim. He had forged the great link that would make possible a Canada stretching from sea to sea.

As the founder of the oldest continuously occupied white
settlement in the province, Fort McLeod, and as the explorer
of the river that bears his name, Fraser must surely rank
as a grandfather both of British Columbia and of
the Canadian federation.

After 1808 . . .

While Fraser was exploring his savage river, Thompson had already explored much of the Columbia. In 1811 he arrived at the Pacific a few months after Astor's overland party had run up to the Stars and Stripes above the first log shelter at Astoria.

Two years later, during the War of 1812, the North West Company shipped its first consignment of trade goods round the Horn. From the mouth of the Columbia, John Stuart explored an inland river-and-pack-horse route to Fort McLeod, New Caledonia, by way of the new Fort Kamloops at the confluence of the north and south branches of the Thompson. That route linked up with Fort Alexandria, also new, on the Fraser between Fort George and the Quesnel River. The first, much-travelled bales reached their destination by this route in the autumn of 1814.

The North West Company merged with the Hudson's Bay Company in 1821. By that time Simon Fraser had retired from his life as a fur trader–explorer, had settled on a farm at St. Andrews, near Cornwall, Ontario, and had married Catherine Macdonell. He lived on his farm until his death in 1862 at the age of eighty-six.

His exploration of the Fraser River received little recognition during his lifetime, the Canadian and British governments deeming it expedient to forget the fur-trade struggles that had opened the entire north-west of the continent to eventual settlement. But the Gold Rush attracted world-wide attention to the river in 1858 and, a few months before the old man's death, his son John Alexander wrote a long letter to the *Hastings Chronicle* that was obviously dictated by the explorer himself. The letter proves that Fraser's mind was still clear and that he was aware of the economic and political significance of the discovery of gold in the Cariboo country. Unhappily for him, his son—and not a grateful country—had to remind the emerging Canada that it was he who through "his exertions and enterprise in all probability secured to the British Crown" the new colony of British Columbia.

As the founder of the oldest continuously occupied white settlement in the province, Fort McLeod, and as the explorer of the river that bears his name, Fraser must surely rank as a grandfather both of British Columbia and of the Canadian federation.

Simon Fraser (1776–1862): A Chronology

The explorer Simon Fraser is remembered mostly for his daring trip down the wild and unforgiving Fraser River in British Columbia, named after him by another famous western explorer, David Thompson.

1776   Born in Vermont, USA.

1784   Immigrated to Canada with widowed mother.

1792   Entered the North West Company of fur traders as an apprentice; his relative, Simon McTavish, was a principal director of the North West Company.

1799   Became an associate of the North West Company.

1804   The XY and North West fur-trading companies amalgamated and continued to explore westward for an inland water route to the Pacific Ocean that would be a cheap and fast means of transporting furs and supplies; Simon Fraser was asked to check out "Mackenzie's river," a route that Mackenzie had discovered, followed, and eventually abandoned because it was too difficult. It was thought this river might be the Columbia River.

1805   Established two trading posts to help supply his exploration trips: the first was at Rocky Mountain Portage House, at the end of the Peace River Canyon, and the second was at Fort McLeod, on Trout Lake, the first permanent white settlement beyond the Rockies.

1806   Ascended the Peace River with a crew, eventually arriving at Stuart Lake, where he built another trading post (Stuart Lake Post/Fort St. James) and then moved on to explore the Fraser River which flowed nearby; he abandoned his first attempt to explore the "savage river" because there was famine in the land and he was unable to acquire food supplies from the local Natives.

1807   Built Fort George (present-day Prince George) where the Nechako River meets the Fraser River and called this area west of the Rockies New Caledonia.

1808   On 28 May, Fraser and 23 others began exploring the Fraser River in four canoes; along the way they faced impossibly wild rapids, equally difficult portages, many Native tribes that were friendly and helpful and some others that were not, until they reached the Strait of Georgia at the river's mouth. He immediately returned to Fort George; the round trip took him 71 days in all. Disappointed that the Fraser River was of no commercial use to the North West Company because it was too ferocious, Fraser did conclude correctly that this was not the famed Columbia River.

1809   Fraser left New Caledonia, but continued to work in the fur trade. He participated in the conflict between the North West Company and the Hudson's Bay Company, and was eventually imprisoned by Lord Selkirk for treason, conspiracy, and accessory to murder.

1817/1818   Fraser was acquitted of all charges. He also left the fur trade to settle in St. Andrews, Ontario, where he married and had eight children.

1862   Fraser died in St. Andrews.

From *Pathfinders and Passageways: The Exploration of Canada* on the National Library of Canada web site (http//nlc-bnc.ca)

*As he looked back from the foot of the rapids while he and
every man crossed themselves and paused to catch their
breath, Fraser knew that here was a cataract that should
always be portaged—if a portage were possible.*

Index

Indians (see Askettih Indians, Atnah Indians, Chilcotin Indians, Cree, Hacamaugh Indians, Lilooet Indians, Musqueam Indians, Salish Indians, Tauten Indians, West Coast Indians)
Iron Rapids, 28

Jackass Mountain, 69, 115
Jefferson, President Thomas, 38

King Charles II, 37
King George III, 133

La Chine, 62
La Vérendrye, 62, 92
Lac La Pluie, 36
Lady Franklin Rock, 75, 78, 81, 83, 110
Lake Superior, 61
Leon Creek, 33, 39, 40, 44, 46, 48, 74, 86, 98, 120, 124, 125, 126
Lewis, Captain Meriwether, 27, 38, 92
Lillooet Indians, 31, 33, 40, 45, 46, 47, 48, 49, 50, 51, 52, 53, 60, 78, 81, 124
   chief, 49, 50, 51
   village, 46, 47, 58, 63, 121, 124
Little Fellow, 63, 71, 72, 74, 83 84, 87, 88, 101, 107, 110, 111, 112, 124, 125, 126, 130
Loch Ness, 137
London, 36, 37, 132, 133
Lord Strathcona, 93
Lytton, 58

Macdonnell, Margaret, 105
Mackenzie, Roderick, 133
Mackenzie, Sir Alexander, 5, 8, 13, 18, 92, 98, 132, 133
McGillivray, William, 37, 48, 38,

66, 134
Métis, 59
Misquiame, 92
Montreal, 4, 6, 8, 10, 37, 38, 70, 85, 88, 104, 120, 121, 132, 136, 139
Musqueam Indians, 86, 87, 93, 94, 95, 96, 97, 105
   village, 92, 94, 96, 110
   warriors, 94

Napoleonic War, 38
Nechako Indians, 138
Nechako River, 9
New Caledonia, 3, 10, 15, 133, 138, 139
New Westminster, 87
New World, 104
New York, 36, 38
Nor'Westers, 9, 37, 38, 60, 62, 137
North West Company, 5, 6, 10, 36, 37, 38, 59, 62, 86, 120, 134, 137, 138, 140

Ottawa River, 25

Pacific Coast, 78, 128
Pacific Ocean, 5, 6, 10, 20, 36, 37, 38, 47, 50, 52, 58, 59, 63, 81, 88, 95, 96, 104, 105, 110, 112, 136, 138, 139
Pacific slope, 3, 8, 17, 19, 59, 63
Parsnip River, 139
Pas-hil-roe, 92
Peace River, 25, 133, 139
   Upper, 3, 5, 61
Pemmican, 15
Perseverence, 6, 8, 9, 32, 39, 86, 126, 133, 139
Pitt River, 83
Portage du Baril, 29, 92, 130

Quesnel, Jules, 3, 8, 9, 13, 16, 29,

30, 39, 53, 68, 84, 93, 103, 105, 106, 115, 117, 121, 136

Quesnel River, 131

Radisson, 62
Rapide Couvert, 29, 31, 33, 49, 129, 130
Rio Grande, 92, 132
Riske Creek, 28
Rocky Mountain House, 61
Rocky Mountains (Rockies), 3, 9, 59, 62

Sac à feu, 6, 85
Salish Indians, 73, 74, 75, 78, 82, 84, 85, 87, 93, 94, 95, 96, 97, 101, 103, 104, 105, 107, 108, 110, 111, 112, 117, 120
  braves, 95
  chief, 85, 86, 96
  guide, 88, 94, 95
  village, 75, 100, 103
Saskatchewan River, 25, 59, 61
Shaw, Angus, 48
Shaw's River, 48
Soda Creek Canyon, 19, 131
Spuzzum, 73, 75
St. Lawrence River, 4, 25, 62
Stave River, 83
Strathglass, Inverness-shire, 104
Strathspey, Scotland, 93
Stuart, John, 3, 6,7, 8, 24, 25, 26, 30, 31, 39, 44, 51, 53, 68, 69, 70, 75, 82, 83, 84, 85, 93, 97, 100, 103, 104, 105, 106, 117, 121, 122, 133, 136, 138
Sumas Peak, 83

Tauten Indians, 18, 19, 24, 33, 36, 49
  chief, 18, 21, 22, 26, 29, 31, 32, 49, 117

guides, 33, 49
The Tours of Dr. Syntax, 133
Thompson River (Thomson's River), 60, 64, 66, 72, 75, 78, 117, 120, 122, 123, 124
Thompson, Charlotte, 59
Thompson, David, 27, 59, 61, 62, 63, 64, 139

Vancouver, Captain, 8, 82
Vermont, 104
Voyages, 133

Wattap, 6, 8, 79
West Coast Indians, 15
West Road River, 13, 132

XY Company, 36, 37

Yale, 78, 108

ABOUT FIFTH HOUSE BOOKS

Fifth House Publishers, a Fitzhenry & Whiteside company, is proudly western-Canadian press. Our publishing specialty non-fiction as we believe that every community must possess positive understanding of its worth and place if it is to remai vital and progressive. Fifth House is committed to "bringing th West to the rest" by publishing approximately twenty books year about the land and people who make this region uniqu Our books are selected for their quality, saleability, and contr bution to the understanding of Western Canadian (an Canadian) history, culture, and environment.

Look for these Western Canadian exploration and adventu books from Fifth House at your favourite bookstore.

*Gully Farm: A Story of Homesteading on the Canadian
    Prairies*, Mary Hiemstra, $14.95
Head-Smashed-In Buffalo Jump, Gordon Reid, $12.95
On the Road with David Thompson, Joyce and Peter McCart
    $18.95
Silk, Spices, and Glory: In Search of the Northwest Passage,
    M. A. Macpherson, $15.95
The Nor'Westers: The Fight for the Fur Trade, by Marjorie
    Wilkins Campbell, $16.95
*The Palliser Expedition: The Dramatic Story of Western
    Canadian Exploration, 1857-1860*, Irene M. Spry, $14.95
The Silent Song: A Tribute to a Reluctant Pioneer Mother, by
    Marjorie Wilkins Campbell $14.95

NOTE: A Teacher's Guide is available at no charge for *The
Savage River*—for more information contact Fitzhenry &
Whiteside 1-800-387-9776.